FEB 1 0 2011

A Journey to Quality Leadership— Quality^3

Also available from ASQ Quality Press:

Out of Another @#&*% Crisis!: Motivation through Humiliation
Mike Micklewright

The Quality Improvement Handbook, Second Edition
John E. Bauer, Grace L. Duffy, and Russell T. Westcott, editors

*The Executive Guide to Understanding and Implementing Employee
Engagement Programs: Expand Production Capacity, Increase Revenue,
and Save Jobs*
Pat Townsend and Joan Gebhardt

*The Certified Manager of Quality/Organizational Excellence Handbook,
Third Edition*
Russell T. Westcott, editor

Mapping Work Processes, Second Edition
Bjørn Andersen, Tom Fagerhaug, Bjørnar Henriksen, and Lars E. Onsøyen

The Quality Toolbox, Second Edition
Nancy R. Tague

*Avoiding the Corporate Death Spiral: Recognizing and Eliminating the
Signs of Decline*
Gregg Stocker

Root Cause Analysis: Simplified Tools and Techniques, Second Edition
Bjørn Andersen and Tom Fagerhaug

*Enabling Excellence: The Seven Elements Essential to Achieving
Competitive Advantage*
Timothy A. Pine

Dare to Be Different!: Reflections on Certain Business Practices
James L. Lamprecht and Renato Ricci

*Office Kaizen: Transforming Office Operations into a Strategic
Competitive Advantage*
William Lareau

An Introduction to Green Process Management
Sam Windsor

To request a complimentary catalog of ASQ Quality Press publications,
call 800-248-1946, or visit our website at http://www.asq.org/quality-press.

A Journey to
Quality Leadership—
Quality³

Lee Mundy

ASQ Quality Press
Milwaukee, Wisconsin

American Society for Quality, Quality Press, Milwaukee 53203
© 2011 by ASQ
All rights reserved. Published 2010
Printed in the United States of America
15 14 13 12 11 10   5 4 3 2 1

Library of Congress Cataloging-in-Publication Data

Mundy, Lee, 1955–.
   A journey to quality leadership: quality[3] / Lee Mundy.
       p. cm.
   Includes bibliographical references and index.
   ISBN 978-0-87389-798-3 (alk. paper)
   1. Quality control.   I. Title.

   TS156.M856 2010
   658.5'62—dc22
                                           2010039202

Publisher: William A. Tony
Acquisitions Editor: Matt Meinholz
Project Editor: Paul O'Mara
Production Administrator: Randall Benson

ASQ Mission: The American Society for Quality advances individual, organiza-
tional, and community excellence worldwide through learning, quality improvement, and knowledge exchange.

Attention Bookstores, Wholesalers, Schools, and Corporations: ASQ Quality Press
books, video, audio, and software are available at quantity discounts with bulk
purchases for business, educational, or instructional use. For information, please
contact ASQ Quality Press at 800-248-1946, or write to ASQ Quality Press,
P.O. Box 3005, Milwaukee, WI 53201-3005.

To place orders or to request a free copy of the ASQ Quality Press Publications
Catalog, visit our website at http://www.asq.org/quality-press.

 Printed on acid-free paper

 Quality Press
600 N. Plankinton Avenue
Milwaukee, Wisconsin 53203
Call toll free 800-248-1946
Fax 414-272-1734
www.asq.org
http://www.asq.org/quality-press
http://standardsgroup.asq.org
E-mail: authors@asq.org

Contents

List of Figures and Tables

Preface

This book is not intended to be an exhaustive dissertation of the many quality tools and processes available today; that is left to authors more scholarly than me. This book is intended to provide a guide or road map to the creation of a comprehensive plan that combines the many tools and strategies that will allow a company to take a quality leadership position.

I have titled this book *A Journey to Quality Leadership— Quality³* because of two incidents I experienced during my many years of working in quality. The first was while I was working as the quality director at a vehicle assembly plant. I had contacted a supplier about the poor quality of his parts, and he stated that the reason for the lack of quality was because I did not understand that in his business, quality was an art, not a science. At that I quickly retorted that if that were the case, then there were no artists at his plant. Looking back, I believe we were both wrong. Quality is not an art, but it must be more than a science. Science typically implies knowledge. Knowledge is not enough. Although how much you know is important, how much you apply is more important. Quality is about execution, about wisdom, about being on a journey to greatness.

The second incident occurred more recently, when I was an engineering director working in quality. My company was making great strides in quality improvement. A dear friend and quality expert in his own right, Shin Taguchi stated that although we were making great strides, we could do better. We needed to visit Japan for a different look at quality, and we needed to institutionalize a culture of quality. I visited Japan with the vice president of engineering, and we hired a man named Tatsuhiko Yoshimura. Tatsuhiko showed me that my quality journey was not over, that significant opportunity still existed by implementing a philosophy entitled "All the People, All the Time" (APAT) and "GD^3" (more about these in later chapters).

The last part of the title, *Quality^3*, helps explain some of the details of the journey. The journey as described in this book includes structure (Five Cs), strategy (focus and APAT), and leadership. I will attempt to detail each part into a comprehensive plan for a successful quality journey. The greatness of your quality journey will be proportional to the volume attained by the product of these three attributes. Obviously, the use of one part will produce a simple line, while the implementation of two parts will constitute a two-dimensional plane that will still have no volume. Implementation of all three will constitute a volume. The greater the implementation of all three, the larger the volume of your quality effort.

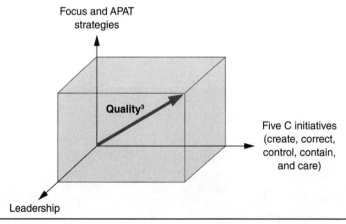

Quality^3: The success of your quality journey will be dependent on the total volume produced by the three contributors.

Quality is a journey, a series of many events that when multiplied together cumulate into a culture that is able to attain and sustain levels of performance that make your customers enthusiastic about your product, your employees passionate about their jobs, and your shareholders excited about their return on their investment. This book reviews not only the knowledge and engineering of quality, but also the wisdom of application.

Quality is also never an accident. Quality is the result of intelligent effort.

Acknowledgments

I deeply appreciate all of the education and support provided by many mentors, especially Dr. Tatsuhiko Yoshimura, Mr. Shin Taguchi, Dr. Subir Chowdhury, Mr. Peter Shainin, and Mr. Don Mitchell. Finally, I would like to thank Mr. Ben Ramnani for his patience in teaching me the basics of quality control.

Introduction

After my college education in engineering, I quickly began a career in engineering within the automotive industry. For the next 10 years I happily went about expanding my engineering experience and knowledge working in product development. Then during the late 1980s I had a wild thought of expanding my career experiences. Looking for a challenging experience, I contemplated working either at a manufacturing plant that struggled in building product or in a sales zone that struggled in selling product. Not knowing anyone in marketing but knowing several plant managers, I pursued the plant job. I thought I had worked out a deal to go to a nearby plant that was performing well. I would work for a few months, have limited responsibilities, and learn about manufacturing. Instead, I was informed that I was to work at a plant 800 miles from my home. This plant was not known for producing high-quality products, and my new job would be quality director. Having never worked in quality or taken any college courses on quality, I expected to be told to read some books, take some classes, and visit some plants that produced quality. Maybe I would even be certified as a quality professional. Instead, I was told "good luck." Since I am not lucky (I have never won anything), I figured I had better find out what it takes to produce quality. I went to the quality library at the plant and checked out a few books, but they contained a lot of theory and very little application. Wanting to find quality applications and usage, I looked into the corporate records to find which plant produced the best quality. At that time the best plant in the corporation was a humble plant in Saltillo, Mexico. So I planned a trip to Saltillo to explore the mysteries of quality. In this plant's quality library I found the same books as at my plant, but the pages in these books had grease on them from so many workers reading them. I then went to the floor and found that management and the workers had taken the learning and were applying it to the production process. They had not only read the books but were using the information to make great products. This life-changing visit to a humble assembly plant began my quality journey. This book is about the lessons I have learned during a journey that began nearly 18 years ago.

Along the way, I have run into many guru-ites. *Guru-ites* are people who worship certain quality philosophies. My journey has taught me that the teachings of one quality expert are insufficient to be a quality leader. Quality leadership requires learning from all the quality masters. From Philip Crosby I learned that the cost of quality is minimal (or free); from W. Edwards Deming I learned that quality is important, obtainable, and more than slogans. From Joseph Juran and Kaoru Ishikawa I learned about the value of and methods for control; from Dorian Shainin I learned the value of the Pareto, statistical problem solving, and the need for statistical confidence. From Genichi Taguchi and Shin Taguchi I learned the value of robustness and societal loss, from Subir Chowdhury I learned the value of quality leadership and business management, and from Tatsuhiko Yoshimura I learned the value of getting an entire organization involved in quality as well as looking at design and validation as opportunities to add value. From Scott Huchingson I learned the value of having the quality strategy formalized in engineering standard work. Finally, from close friend Don Mitchell I learned about having a passion for quality. I owe any success

I might have to the giants who came before me and established the quality processes and strategies.

For you, a perfect picture of quality may be classical music from a high-fidelity tuner while you rest in your easy chair. For me, a perfect picture of great quality is a superb vehicle on a winding road on a cloud-free day. For this reason, I will carefully define over a number of chapters the pieces that make up that picture.

I hope you enjoy reading this book as much as I have enjoyed my quality journey.

PART I
Quality Basics

1

What Is Quality?

In this chapter we will see what quality is and what its most significant contributors are. In addition, we will look at the benefits of emphasizing great quality and the liabilities of neglecting quality.

The *American Heritage Dictionary* defines quality as "the essential character of something, an inherent or distinguishing character, or superiority of kind." The American Society for Quality (ASQ) defines quality as "the totality of features and characteristics of a product that bear on its ability to satisfy given needs."

Quality is most often talked about in the negative. Very few people talk about having an abundance of quality, but almost everyone talks about the lack of it. Lack of quality can be observed daily, whether it is the MP3 player that will not keep a charge, the cell phone that loses its signal, the cap on the soda bottle that leaks, or the vehicle that hesitates and stalls. Lack of quality is a topic everyone agrees with and is passionate about. It is also one of the key reasons a customer changes brands. Due to the broad discussions on quality, most people believe they know what is required to produce quality products. For companies that are not at the top of the quality pyramid, the common logic is that if they had just a little more time, a little more money, or a little more manpower, they too would have great quality. Many companies persist in spending money and manpower while losing valuable time and customers to their competitors. In other cases, companies look for a silver bullet, something that will solve all of their quality concerns. These companies float from initiative to initiative without ever fully implementing a comprehensive strategy. In reality, very few companies actually have the knowledge required to produce great quality. Even fewer companies have the drive and wisdom to obtain quality leadership.

Quality is the absolute fulfillment of a customer's expectations. In the past, quality was primarily about the absence of things gone wrong. As products continue to improve and failures diminish, this characterization of quality has changed to include a new definition: the abundance of things gone right. Quality is having pride of ownership and complete trust and satisfaction in the product you have invested your savings in.

Some companies have created a reputation for great quality, allowing them to charge a premium for the products they sell. Great quality generates great customer loyalty. Even if your company does not have the desire to produce the best quality, you can still make significant improvements in quality to at least keep your current customers.

Quality has a significant impact on the bottom line. No company can stay in business long without profits, and no company can be profitable for long without having great quality. You may be able to identify some companies that have poor quality and have stayed in business, but I think you will find that there are few. Most companies with poor quality are dying a very slow death or have monopolies by legislative or business requirements. Profitability is driven by market share, high unit profit, and low material and production costs. These in turn are driven by quality.

In a mature market, the equation for market share is quite simple: It is driven by customer loyalty and customer conquest.

Loyalty is the ability to keep your customers buying your products (and not your competitors' products), and conquest is the ability to take customers away from your competitors.

Let's look at each factor individually, starting with loyalty. The biggest influence on loyalty is the experiences the customer has during the life of the product, but most importantly during the final months before a new purchase. If those final experiences have been good, the customer is more inclined to repeat that experience with a product from the same manufacturer. As a matter of fact, some customers feel the product takes on the personal characteristics of a family member. One of the first cars I owned was such a great vehicle I felt guilty selling it at 160,000 miles. I felt as though I was selling a member of the family. On the opposite side, if the experience has been bad, the customer feels no allegiance to the manufacturer. Loyalty is driven by the number (and cost) of failures experienced in the final period of ownership. Using a personal computer as an illustration, an owner may become accustomed to some slowness or occasional glitches and may accept a few insignificant problems. But the owner will rarely accept numerous problems or significant, expensive failures.

Some manufacturers have maintained loyalty through patriotism, using slogans such as "Buy American." Although this practice can be beneficial, it is not sustainable. Your customers will become accustomed to your competitors, even if your competitors are foreign. Over time, your competitors will become familiar and thus "Americanized." In addition, many of your competitors have begun manufacturing, assembly, and even engineering processes within the United States.

The second factor of generating additional market share is through conquest. Conquest is the ability to take a customer away from another manufacturer. Conquest is driven by styling, cost, magazine and newspaper articles, published quality reports, and showroom quality.

Let's review the factors that drive conquest. First, few people will buy ugly products (well, people with questionable taste do, but don't rely on them for your long-term future). I am extremely left-brained and know absolutely nothing about styling; on this subject, you are on your own.

On pricing I do know a little. Nobody will throw money away on an overpriced product. Although your pricing may be in line with your development, production, and quality costs, it may still be too high. As you learned in your college economics class, the price is set by the market. If the market price is below the price you have set for a sustainable return, you had better find out how to reduce your price quickly. This is a double-edged sword: Reducing your price may increase your market share but reduce your per-unit profits. Conversely, increasing your price may increase per-unit profit but reduce your market share. The best solution is to reduce your costs while you increase your product's value. Many factors contribute to the cost and value of a product; unfortunately, few people realize the significance of the cost and value of quality (or better described as the cost of low quality).

One of your major cost factors that must be figured into the price is the cost of quality. This cost is typically broken into external (customer identified) and internal (producer identified) costs. Although this breakdown of costs is historical and reasonable, it does not necessarily provide good direction to the different functions within a corporation for reducing quality costs. Perhaps a better breakdown is to lump quality costs associated with production and control versus quality costs associated with design and engineering. Reducing the production and control portions of quality costs can be achieved by reducing the need for and the amount of inspection, sorting, rework, and scrappage. Additionally, the design and engineering portions of quality costs can be significantly reduced by the use of quality tools during design and development of the product.

A side benefit of reducing quality costs is the associated reduction of productivity costs. Improving production quality (reducing production quality costs) also increases production and reduces its associated costs. Improving engineering quality can potentially reduce product cost, mass, and development time. Most of the tools used are not just quality tools but optimization tools. The use of Pugh analysis, Design for Six Sigma (DFSS), design of experiments (DOE), design failure modes and effects analysis (DFMEA), and the like can not only reduce the number of potential failures but also reduce the mass and price of the individual systems that make up your product.

Finally, for many big-ticket items such as homes and vehicles, the price the customer sees is not just the initial price but the residual value of the product. Residual value is driven by people willing to pay a premium for your used product. If the quality is good, the residual value remains high. If the product retains its value over time, the customer can sell the product at a future date and purchase your new model using those savings. Products also have a time value associated with technology. Because of rapid advances in technology, products such as computers, TVs, and cell phones do not typically have high residual values. A pseudo residual value may be the value associated with the willingness of customers to repurchase the same brand without additional marketing.

Besides price (or cost), conquest is also driven by what your potential customers read about your product in numerous magazines and newspapers and on websites. Endorsements and approvals by product testing and rating groups can often produce significant sales gains. Product testing and rating groups typically have a series of performance tests they run on a large number of products grouped within several categories. Many testing companies also send out surveys asking their readers for their likes and dislikes as well as the number and types of failures their various products experience. Magazine articles and other published reports can provide the benefit of free advertising as long as their publishers say good things about your product. Remember, these articles are usually written from experiences with early production or even prototype products. Therefore, you must make sure you are just as proud of your first products as you are of those a year or two in production. If any magazine or testing company has a larger influence than others on what your customers buy, get close to that company. Find out its likes and dislikes and never argue with anyone from that company (remember the saying of Mark Twain, "Never get in an argument with someone who buys ink by the barrel"). Look to their point of view; it may have merit. If you have some logical arguments, share them. If you can't agree and you feel you are in the right, stick by your ideas.

I often hear complaints about testing companies and how their write-ups are unfair. When I have investigated, I have found that although the testing companies had some biases in their likes and dislikes, most often the issues identified were the same as those that the customers identified. Testing companies also have customers, and if the companies do a poor job of representing their customers, they may lose them. I have concluded that if a testing company's endorsement means that much to me, I had better look at its thoughts more earnestly.

Continuing with conquest, showroom quality is the quality a customer can see on the showroom floor; it's about features, layout, appearance, fits, and visual defects. Showroom quality applies to all products. If the potential customer likes what he or she sees, then he or she may go the second step and evaluate it. If you manufacture vehicles, your potential customer may want to test drive your vehicle, where acceleration, smoothness of ride, and noise are evaluated. If your product is electronic, your customer may want to plug it in or play it. Your customer will be looking for performance at high volume or weak signal strength. High showroom quality provides the opportunity to demonstrate performance quality, which might provide the opportunity and impact to move to a sale of the product.

Quality is more than just the lack of things gone wrong. Quality today is becoming even more about subliminal excitement or the abundance of things gone right. I lump "things gone right" into what I call perceived quality. Perceived quality is often subliminal: You may not be able to put your finger on it, but you sure know how it feels in your gut. Perceived quality can be broken down into four categories: humanity, consistency, integrity, and subliminal excitement.

Humanity is the ability to use a product the way you desire, not necessarily the way the manufacturer intended. If you manufacture power tools, it is the ease of handling the tool, the torque and speed of the tool, and the understandability of tool settings and features. If you manufacture cell phones, it is the ability to read and use the buttons and controls. If you manufacture and sell vehicles, it is the ability to easily get into and out of your product, the stowability of the seats, and the placement and extent of cup holders and storage compartments. In humanity you must discern the voice of the customer from the voice of the engineer. I often hear from engineers who are frustrated because customers complain about and malign features and options that are working exactly as the engineers intended. I keep reminding these engineers that success is not measured by how well the system they created satisfies their creative and engineering abilities; rather, success is measured by how well the needs and wants of the customer are satisfied.

Consistency is the continuity between your product and other products the customer comes into contact with. For example, zone heating/cooling in your house could lead to a discussion of why zone climate control is not available in your vehicle. Consistency is also about constancy within your product. For electronic products, are the buttons and controls consistent? Are the size, feel, and shape of the buttons consistent? Are the efforts on all the buttons consistent? If not, do the inconsistencies make sense and are they easily understood by the customer? I have seen some products, specifically vehicles, where the features and controls were significantly different. It looked as though many parts and systems were sourced from many suppliers, with no conversation among them or with engineering. Some vehicles had a wide variety of interior colors and interior texture grains and glosses with no perceived rhyme or reason. Buttons for the radio and the air conditioning were different sizes and shapes, and all had significantly different efforts. Why did these differences exist? Would the differences make sense to the customer, or would they cause confusion? Inconsistencies such as these may confuse the customer and lead to feelings of poor quality.

Integrity is about the various systems performing the way the customer expects. Many portable CD and DVD players have various systems to control skips. If the customer pays for these features, do they work? I often hear about customers having problems with their CD players not playing CDs that they created. Again, the engineer may not have comprehended all CD formats, but the customer still expects to play CDs in any player.

The last perceived quality feature is subliminal excitement. This form of quality takes the product beyond expectations. Dr. Noriaki Kano of Japan has written much about three types of needs: excitement, performance, and basic (see Figure 1.1). He calls his highest needs "excitement needs" (what I call subliminal excitement). Subliminal excitement causes the customer to say "Wow!" All three of Dr. Kano's needs must be satisfied for high quality, but only subliminal excitement has the tremendous ability to conquest sales.

A study I was involved in many years ago looked at two nearly identical vehicles that had significantly different levels of customer satisfaction. The customer satisfaction on one vehicle was 25%–30% higher than on the other vehicle. Both vehicles were built on the same assembly line, both had the

A product needs a balance of excitement, performance, and basic needs. Excitement needs will eventually become performance needs and then basic needs as they become increasingly common.

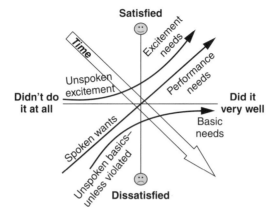

For example, early telephones were hardwired to the wall, and party lines of multiple users having the same phone number were common. Today, cell phones are full of basic functions that were at one time exciters. Features such as web access, still photography, voice recording, and GPS tracking were all excitement needs when first introduced.

Constant innovation is required to maintain leadership.

Figure 1.1   Kano model.

same number of problems, and both had the same styling and paint colors. Under further analysis, two features produced the significant customer satisfaction offset: a turbo-charged engine and leather interior.

In both cases, vehicle performance, vehicle acceleration, and the richness of the interior far exceeded the customers' expectations. Likewise, text messaging and cameras in cell phones have brought significant customer enthusiasm. In the future these features will be basic, and customers will be looking for video conferencing. An additional example of subliminal excitement comes from the auto industry. Almost all vehicles have warning lights and tones that respond when your fuel is low. But in some vehicles, a message appears in the driver information center asking if you would like the location of all gas stations to be shown on the navigation system. Not only does the vehicle tell you it is getting low on fuel, but it tells you where to go to fill up. I can remember when the low-fuel light was an exciter (I guess this shows my age).

Another example is vehicle telematics, such as OnStar from General Motors. With this system, if a vehicle crash occurs and the airbags are deployed, OnStar calls the driver to confirm whether anyone in the vehicle has been injured. If injuries have occurred or if there is no response, OnStar calls emergency personnel and sends them to the appropriate location.

Human nature is such that today's customer enthusiasm is tomorrow's general expectation. All of those features and performance characteristics that are so exciting today will be expected in your product tomorrow. Remember, the loyalty and conquest game is played by all of your competitors. Make sure you play with a complete hand.

Let's look at a puzzle analogy. Quality is not the individual puzzle pieces but the total picture. For me, the picture is made up of three parts: the great vehicle, the road the vehicle is being driven on, and the location and landscape of the road (see Figure 1.2).

No amount of imagination could ever produce a great picture if the vehicle is a rusted-out junker traveling on a straight, broken-down asphalt highway through a rundown industrial waste area of a city. All three qualities are required to make up the great experience.

The great picture is the product of the great vehicle, the great road, and the great location. If any part is missing, greatness will be lacking. Most quality plans look exclusively at the individual puzzle pieces (tools and strategies) and do not comprehend the connectivity and arrangement of the pieces. The quality plan outlined in this book (and the picture that will be produced) includes great strategies, great initiatives, and great

Great vehicle

Great road

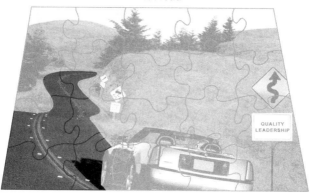

Great location

Figure 1.2 Three puzzle pieces of the quality driving experience.

leadership. Although the picture cannot be produced without the puzzle pieces, we should never take our eye off the final product, which is the great picture being produced and the joy we have when it is achieved.

> *Quality is more than the elimination of "things gone wrong." It is the creation of "things gone right." Quality is the combination of no defects with purposeful attention to making products understandable, usable, and in harmony with other products. Quality is about achieving a new level of excitement and achieving customer satisfaction and enthusiasm in an ever-increasing manner. Failure to provide this level of customer passion may encourage your customers to look at your competitors' products and send you down the road to extinction.*

ADDITIONAL READING

Kano, N., N. Seraku, F. Takahaahi, and S. Tsuji. 1984. "Attractive Quality and Must-Be Quality." [In Japanese.] *Journal of the Japanese Society for Quality Control* 14(2):147–156.

2

Basic Quality Understanding

This chapter reviews basic quality principles.

To be the best in quality requires knowledge and application from many sources. I believe there are three primary categories of this knowledge. The first area of expertise is from the quality experts who have spent their lives establishing quality principles and practices. Hundreds, if not thousands, of quality books have been published, documenting in great detail the activities that need to be completed to produce quality. Much of the great work by the quality masters has been written over the last 30 to 40 years. Many universities now have significant quality curricula that teach the fundamentals as well as specific and advanced quality tools and strategies.

The second source of learning comes from your competitors and/or other engineering and manufacturing companies. Your competitors may have many unique quality ideas and applications (especially if they have better quality than your company). Knowledge and application of the best practices of these companies can be a shortcut to significantly improved quality. To institutionalize your competitors' best practices, make sure you *fully understand* all actions as well as the logic and reasoning behind each step. To be successful you must have this understanding of your competitors' culture, historical learning, training, and support. Textbooks are full of case studies of companies that have been unsuccessful in trying to copy their competitors' solutions without the knowledge of their culture, training, and so forth. A great example is the attempt by many companies to implement Japanese-style quality circles in the 1970s. Quality circles were and are successfully used by Japanese companies, but they have experienced limited success in the United States due to the lack of team culture that is commonplace in Japan. Remember that while duplicating your competitors' practices can greatly reduce the distance to their quality level, you can rarely surpass their quality only by mimicking them.

The final source of expertise is you and the others in your company with great quality ideas. If you look around your company, you will find significant quality initiatives and practices. In many cases, these initiatives are unique to your company. When visiting different companies, I am constantly amazed by great quality initiatives that are unique to the company or are significant modifications of more recognized initiatives. If you can harness and institutionalize the initiatives of your employees, you can extend the distance from your competitor or at least close some of the quality gap.

I have identified the teachings of the experts as one of the sources of learning, but it is probably the most significant. The experts who have radically changed the science of quality are Crosby, Deming, Juran, Taguchi (Genichi and Shin), Wu, Ishikawa, Chowdhury, Shainin, Yoshimura, and others (I apologize to those I may have left out). These experts (and the others) have written extensively on the strategies and disciplines required to produce great quality.

In addition to the writings of the great quality leaders, books and/or technical papers may have been documented by your competitors and others in your business who have implemented the principles of these masters. Even if competitor practices are not documented, you may still gain knowledge of their initiatives. They may be willing to share practices and initiatives with you as a common industry courtesy or in some form of reciprocity (they may ask you to share some of your systems at the same time). Common suppliers may also give insight into your competitors' best practices.

If your expectations are more immediate or you have been less than successful in implementing competitor practices, you may want to hire some of your competitor's quality leaders. You may have to swallow some pride and be humble in seeking out greatness from your competitor, but remember the goal. Being the best will have benefits far beyond the momentary loss of pride when asking for help.

Regrettably, the last category mentioned is often the most overlooked: the ideas from within your company. When you start looking around, you may be surprised by the large number of great initiatives that can be found at the grassroots level. Often companies hire consultants at great expense when potential strategies and processes already exist within reach and can be harnessed with some direct leadership. You may have to be creative in seeking out the best practices and then institutionalizing them. Remember, you are not the only person in your company who desires the company to be great. Most of your employees are striving for the same goal.

With these three contributors of knowledge, shown in Figure 2.1, your company can obtain the *knowledge* to overtake your competitors in quality. If your company also has strong

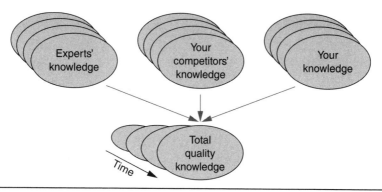

Figure 2.1 Three primary contributors of knowledge.

leadership, with the drive to be the best, you can command quality leadership.

I started my quality journey with very little knowledge of quality. Thirty years ago there were very few quality classes taught at any university. Most quality discussions were centered on manufacturing. Within engineering, the primary discussion was centered on performance, with only secondary discussions on quality and failures. When I was transferred to an assembly plant, I realized that for me to contribute to the plant's improvement in quality, I had better learn all I could about quality. My first observation was that some plants produced great quality, while others continually struggled. By doing a little investigating I found that there was one plant that was always producing the highest quality. This plant was not only at the top, but by a significant margin. It's interesting to note that this plant was not the closest to headquarters, the newest, or full of college graduates trained in quality. The plant was a humble operation in Mexico that was dedicated to producing quality and was led by quality expert Peter Dersley. I quickly got on a plane and visited this quality mecca. During my visit I easily identified why the plant was great: the engineers and operators had read the quality manuals and were doing what the manuals suggested. At our plant, we had a quality library but it was rarely used. This Mexican plant had the same books, but they were covered in dirt and grease from being read by the employees, who put the recommendations into practice. This was one of my first lessons: If you plan on being great in quality, you must first understand quality and then put into practice what you have learned.

The book of Proverbs talks about knowledge, understanding, and wisdom. Knowledge is about facts and data. It is achieved through your experiences and/or information obtained through reading or instruction. Understanding is about comprehension, appreciation, and insight. It is about comprehending what needs to be done with the knowledge.

Wisdom is about application and about institutionalizing corrective actions on the basis of your knowledge and understanding (see Figure 2.2). Many people have knowledge of quality, fewer people know how to apply their learning, and even fewer actually get the opportunity or have the leadership capabilities to implement the principles of quality. To be the best in quality you must put your learning into practice. To be successful in your quality journey you will have to read about quality, visit where application is occurring, and drive implementation within an organization that may not be eager to change.

Your quality journey (like any trip you take) contains three parts: your destination, your transportation, and the resources to complete the trip (see Figure 2.3).

Your *destination* is the quality expectations of your company. Hopefully, your company has the desire to be the best in its field. This goal is the first and often the most important step

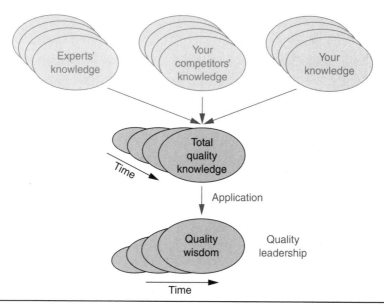

Figure 2.2   Quality knowledge to quality wisdom by application.

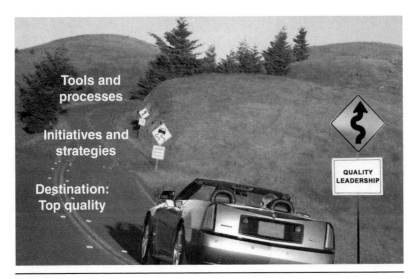

Figure 2.3   Quality journey.

in your drive to a new level of customer satisfaction. This goal must not be a casual identification of a lofty target; it must be a rigorous communication of an achievable objective, supported by senior leadership. If your company does not have the desire to be the highest-quality producer, then it will probably achieve its goal of mediocrity.

The *means of transportation* in the analogy are your quality initiatives and strategies. These strategies should be based on the profound understanding of what is required to create and improve the quality of your products.

Lastly, the *resources* to complete the trip are the tools and processes that make up your strategies. Hundreds of processes are available; some are extremely beneficial, and some are only somewhat beneficial. Match your needs and company culture with the processes that provide the greatest benefits.

Your destination is to be the best in quality. No other destination is acceptable. If your expectations are not to be the best, you can stop reading this book; besides a few interesting stories, it will be of little benefit to you. Being the best dominates conversations and drives all competition to compare against you (constantly being identified as the best by your competitors also provides considerable free advertising). Being the best eliminates the need for explanations and excuses. Being the best opens doors to higher profits and increased market share. Being the best is critical to a winning strategy. As Vince Lombardi talked about, winning is not the most important thing, it is the only thing. Everyone in your organization must recognize the goals your company has established. For that reason, this destination must be broadcast frequently and enthusiastically by all top leaders. Always remember, in this game all ties go to the current winner. If you are currently in second place, do not celebrate when you equal your competition; celebrate when you are finally ahead of your competition. As the great quality leader Guy Briggs always said, "Celebrate on the run, because the race never ends."

Your strategies should be broken down into APAT and focus strategies. Your initiatives should be broken down into five categories, which I call the Five Cs: care, contain, control, correct, and create. These five categories are characterized by the speed of implementation, amount of improvement, level of difficulty, and implementation owner. Upcoming chapters will be dedicated to each of these categories of strategies and initiatives.

Finally, your tools and processes are the actions taken within each improvement category. These tools and their application demonstrate the quality wisdom your company has obtained. These tools are DFSS, statistical engineering and Red X, failure modes and effects analysis (FMEA), quality function deployment (QFD), design review based on failure mode (DRBFM), design review based on test results (DRBTR), process control, and many others to be described later.

Your quality journey will not occur overnight, but it can begin tomorrow. The journey may be measured in years, although you should see improvement in weeks. On the journey you will experience bumps and detours. *Do not* attempt to implement all tools and strategies simultaneously. Different strategies require different skills. The employees developing new products will use the creation strategies, and the current production employees will use the improvement strategies. Keep your focus on the destination and do not get distracted. Learn, interact, and have fun.

Obtaining quality requires knowledge, understanding, and wisdom. Knowledge is easily obtained through reading the works of the quality masters as well as the technical papers within the many industrial associations. Understanding is obtained through observing the quality practices of high-quality producers. Wisdom is obtained through the application of strong leadership. As the book of Proverbs states, "For wisdom is more precious than rubies, and nothing you desire can compare with her."

PART II

Quality Strategies

3

Focus Strategies

This chapter discusses and reviews focus strategies. The benefits and liabilities of driving quality improvement with focus strategies will be reviewed as well as the identification of some common focus strategies.

Quality strategies typically fall into two categories: focus strategies and "all the people, all the time" strategies (from here on, referred to as APAT strategies). These two categories have significantly different philosophies, purposes, and uses. Focus strategies involve creating Pareto charts and working on the major Pareto contributors with your best and brightest resources. APAT strategies involve work on all concerns with the entire workforce. Stated differently, the focus strategies look at the left side of the Pareto (the tall bars), while the APAT strategies look at the whole Pareto (all the bars). Companies in North America and Europe primarily use focus strategies, and Japanese companies primarily use APAT strategies. American manufacturing usage of the APAT strategies has been less extensive. Applying both strategies may offer an opportunity to close the gap further or even pass your competitors' quality.

The Pareto principle is often called the 80/20 principle. It is a powerful principle that declares that 80% of the output can be achieved by 20% of the effort. For most Western cultures, the Pareto principle has been ingrained in our thought process since preschool. In our adolescent gym classes we were often required to line up, tallest to shortest, for the selection of teams (typically with the thought that the tallest athletes produced the greatest effort and therefore needed to be balanced with the vertically impaired students). In high school we learned that 80% of our term paper could be written with 20% of the effort. For some, the remaining 20% was not worth the effort, and we accepted a mediocre grade. Finally, when we became adults and started to generate "to do" lists, we quickly figured out that 80% of the projects could be completed with 20% of the effort.

Many companies follow Pareto analysis and focus strategies extensively. These companies regularly maintain a top issues list or a top 20 list. Numerous companies keep a "rolling top 5" that draw company-wide support and executive reviews. Nearly all companies have expert problem-solving teams to work on the most significant and difficult problems (see Figure 3.1).

Focus strategies *can* (and usually do) bring significant and rapid quality improvements. Unfortunately, these quick improvements can result in premature optimism about achieving quality leadership. Long-term reliance on *only* the Pareto

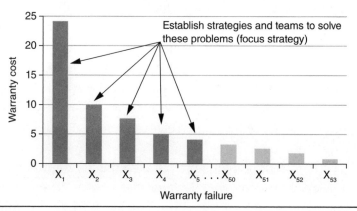

Figure 3.1   Pareto principle.

principle and focus strategies can lead to a deceleration in your quality improvement rate. As you continue to work only on the left side of the Pareto chart, these tall bars will get smaller and smaller. After some time the Pareto will lose its characteristic shape (it will flatten), and the contribution of these systems or concerns will be reduced. When this happens, your future quality improvement rates will be significantly reduced.

These reduced quality improvement rates often lead to much soul-searching and finger-pointing about the cause of the slowdown in quality improvement. The focus strategy is not broken; it has just lost its effectiveness.

All strategies move on a path called a logistic curve, or what I call a "strategy effectiveness curve" (see Figure 3.2). The horizontal axis identifies the time from the initiation of the strategy, and the vertical axis identifies the value added by the strategy. The introduction of strategies follows a fairly regular pattern and includes periods of great growth and periods of stagnation.

All strategies start in a slow growth period called the *incubation period*. During the incubation period we get our first indications of the success of the strategy. The incubation period can take from several months to several years. In the early 1990s my company started using Red X problem solving, often

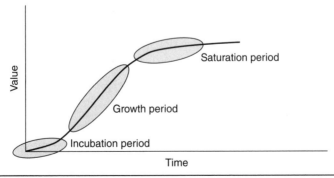

Figure 3.2 Strategy effectiveness curve (logistic curve).

called the Shainin Problem Solving Method (we shall call it statistical engineering for the rest of the book). The incubation period took several years to get sufficient success stories to generate corporate buy-in. One of the key lessons gained during the incubation period is that success is measured not by how many people have been trained in the strategy, but by how many people are using the strategy successfully. In my experience with the rollout of the statistical engineering strategy, too much effort was initially consumed teaching large groups of people about it. Unfortunately, most of the people trained were not in a position to use the strategy. To get the most out of the training during the incubation period, make sure that only the people who will be executing or applying the strategy and those who directly support those practicing engineers are trained. Also, make sure everyone who is trained has an active project and sufficient time allocated to work on the new strategy. All engineers involved in a new strategy or tool must have their current responsibilities removed or significantly reduced so that they can fully concentrate on the new strategy or tool.

Not everyone will be pleased with having to implement new strategies. Therefore, look for anyone trying to sabotage the new tools and strategies. Although questions and comments can be beneficial in the successful rollout of a new tool, blind criticism can be detrimental. In my case, a coworker called the company awareness line, a hotline set up to report company fraud, to report me. Although I never experienced a day with the corporate auditors, and I had no trouble convincing them that I was not trying to sabotage the company, I would not want to experience that again.

The first successes of a new strategy lead to accelerated development and implementation of the strategy. This portion of the logistic curve is called the *growth period*. It is during this period that the strategy starts producing significant quality improvements. The first successes quickly lead to more training, which leads to more execution, which leads to more success. Regrettably, as success eliminates problems and improves quality, the remaining opportunities are less significant. This is called "elimination of the low-hanging fruit." When all the low-hanging fruit has been picked (the tall bars on the left side of the Pareto chart have been eliminated), the success of the strategy is reduced, and we hit what is called the *saturation period.* During the saturation period, sustained improvement rates can only be achieved by finding ways to re-create the Pareto chart or by bringing in significantly more problem solvers. During the saturation period, more and more resources get fewer and fewer results. This reduced output is not due to the value of your people or the goodness of your strategy; it is due to the fact that your strategy is a focus strategy and your Pareto is becoming flat. This is great news—your strategy has been working. Unfortunately, this news also brings challenges.

As you work the Pareto, its shape will change. Over time, the Pareto will lose its characteristic tall bars on the left side and will be replaced with a chart that shows very little discrimination from the left to the right side of the graph. As the Pareto chart flattens, you can either continue working on the top few issues, which will lower your problem-solving effectiveness, or reconstruct the Pareto (if possible) to redefine clear contrasts. One such way to reconstruct the Pareto is by changing what is measured. Typically, Pareto charts are created by plotting failure parts versus failure frequency. Some gains can be achieved by plotting failure mode versus failure frequency. Although you may have hundreds of similar parts that fail (from the numerous products that you sell), they may have only a couple of common failure modes. An example could be in electrical connectors. Engineers commonly plot the failure of each connector and then fix the worse connectors. Since there may be 200–400 connectors within a large system (such as an appliance or vehicle), using a Pareto chart can keep problem solvers busy for some time. Unfortunately, once the worse connectors are fixed, you now have a Pareto that is 300 bars wide and has very few differences in height. In geographic terms, you have a lake that is 10 miles wide and 2 inches deep. An alternate strategy would be to switch from failure parts to failure modes. In this case, the connectors have two failure modes: (1) the connector comes apart (separates into two halves), and (2) connectivity within the connector is lost (but the connector halves stay together). After plotting the failure modes, you now have a Pareto with 2 bars rather than 300 bars, and significant problem solving can be resumed. Again in geographic terms, your lake has returned to ½ mile wide and 300 feet deep.

Figure 3.3 shows the Pareto when you first start the focus strategy (light gray bars) and after a passage of time executing the strategy (dark gray bars). As can be seen, the Pareto has lost its characteristic tall bars on the left. If in the example you had allocated resources to only the top five failures and you get a percentage improvement for each of these failures, it can be easily calculated that your return will decrease significantly over time.

The attributes of focus strategies are many: (1) They are driven by key people or groups with extremely high skill levels, (2) they use complex or very technical tools, (3) problem solving takes considerable time due to the complexity of the

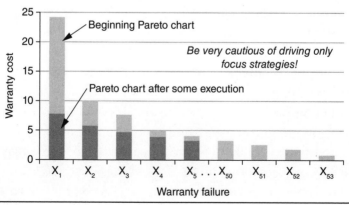

Figure 3.3 Quality strategies.

tools and the magnitude of the issue, and (4) focus strategies recognize and reward individuals as heroes.

Some extremely beneficial focus strategies are the following: focused problem solving, statistical engineering, DFSS, and a rolling top issues list. Any strategy that is started with the thought of creating a Pareto is a focus strategy. If a Pareto can be created, a focus strategy would be beneficial.

Although focus strategies are most often applied to correction, I will spend some time in the upcoming chapters talking about focus strategies in each of the five C initiatives.

> *Driving focus strategies can provide quick and effective quality improvements. Tools and problem solvers can be directed at some of your largest problems, and results can be obtained quickly. Driving focus strategies can quickly eliminate the quality gap with your competitor. Unfortunately, relying only on focus strategies will lead to stagnation and diminishing quality returns over time, and continued reliance will reduce your ability to beat your competitor in quality.*

ADDITIONAL READING

Bhote, K. R., and A. Bhote. 2000. *World Class Quality: Using Design of Experiments to Make It Happen.* New York: American Management Association.

Koch, R. 2008. *The 80/20 Principle: The Secret to Success by Achieving More with Less.* New York: Doubleday.

4

"All the People, All the Time" Strategies

This chapter discusses and reviews APAT strategies. The benefits and liabilities of driving quality improvement with APAT strategies will be reviewed as well as the identification of some common APAT strategies.

The quality strategies and tools your company is using, or is investigating for use, are extremely important. One of the great failures of the Western quality movement is the frequent belief that success can be achieved by a small percentage of the workforce driving the latest initiatives, tools, or procedures. A key quality lesson I learned, unfortunately later in my career, is that without the engagement of your entire workforce, you will struggle to compete with any competitor that has its entire workforce engaged, even if your strategies are more robust.

The actor Will Smith was interviewed by *Reader's Digest* for the December 2006 issue. In the article he was asked what kept him ahead of other actors. Will stated that he gave 100% of his effort, 100% of the time. Although he did not win every battle, in the end he won against the individual who gave only 87% effort, 60% of the time. Smith's knowledge also applies to companies. While the company that gives 87% may win a number of battles with its competitor, in the end it can never win the war against the company that gives 100% of the effort, 100% of the time, by 100% of the staff.

The quality policy of many companies has relied on driving the latest quality strategy and initiatives with the most rigorous implementation rules and responsibilities. These companies typically look for the "latest *best*" strategy and procedure. They are in search of that silver bullet that will eliminate their quality problems. Often these companies have the best and latest quality tools.

Tatsuhiko Yoshimura has taught me that great tools and supporting systems by themselves often tend to make it appear unnecessary to "go and see" the real world and to "think and worry" about quality. Many companies also try to identify responsibilities down to the lowest level in the organization. If your rules and responsibilities are too well defined, it may give the impression that quality is for other people to worry about.

Companies that produce great quality do not always have the latest tools and strategies. Instead, many of these companies rely on engagement of their entire workforce. This total engagement of the workforce is the strength of the APAT strategies. APAT strategies involve the engagement of all employees, looking for quality opportunities, all the time.

In Figure 4.1, I compare the "typical" company with the "better" company. "Better" companies draw their quality improvement not from the greatness in their strategies and processes but from the engagement of the total workforce on quality.

In the "typical" company, you would observe a small group of quality experts rolling out grand strategies on how to beat the competition (typically following focus strategies). But in the "better" company, you would observe engineers calling retailers and customers and working late at night within a team correcting the issues identified within their systems.

If a company has all the people engaged, all the time, and is also applying the best APAT and focus strategies, it can have

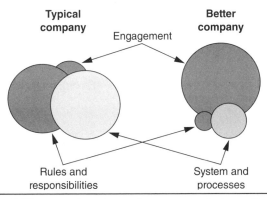

Figure 4.1 Differences in cultures between typical quality and better quality companies.

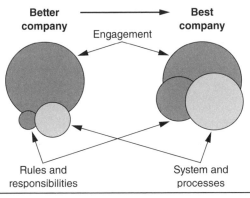

Figure 4.2 Differences in cultures between better quality and best quality companies.

an advantage over even the present "better" company. "Best" companies have all of their people engaged in driving quality and are also driving improvement through the latest of tools and strategies (see Figure 4.2).

The key principle is that a company's strategies and initiatives are important, but they are not totally effective unless they are applied by all the people, all the time. Only after the entire workforce is engaged can you reap the benefits of more defined processes and responsibilities.

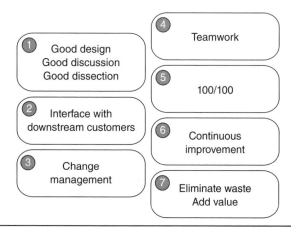

Figure 4.3   The seven disciplines of APAT.

APAT is made up of seven distinct disciplines, as described by Tatsuhiko Yoshimura (see Figure 4.3). The first discipline is called *Good design, good discussion, and good dissection*, or GD³. GD³ is about looking at the product development process as an opportunity to add value and reduce the possibility of unplanned problems. The second discipline is *Interface with your downstream customers*. Great designs require healthy communication and respect between upstream and downstream processes. The third discipline is *Change management*. All changes create opportunities for unforeseen problems to emerge; care must be taken to control change to minimize problems. The fourth discipline is *Teamwork*. Winning requires teamwork. Although individual efforts are required, the cooperation and discipline of teamwork is required to win. The fifth discipline is *100/100*. To win requires everyone (100% of the organization) devoting every minute (100% of the time) to winning. The sixth discipline is *Continuous improvement*. Opportunities always exist, and continuous improvement must be used to consistently move to higher quality levels. The seventh and final discipline is the *Elimination of waste and the addition of value*. Always look to eliminate all waste within the process of design, and at the same time look for means of adding value to each activity.

Let's look at each discipline in more detail. The first APAT discipline, *Good design, good discussion, and good dissection (GD³),* is centered on using multiple design reviews to enable teams to *visualize problems before they have a chance to occur.* The Japanese word for visualizing problems before their outbreak is *Mizenboushi.* To my knowledge, the first person to write and lecture about Mizenboushi was Tatsuhiko Yoshimura. Unfortunately, his book *Mizenboushi Method—GD³* is currently published only in Japanese, by JUSE Press. The design reviews described by Yoshimura are centered on good designs, good discussions, and good dissection. The comprehensive goal of GD³ is to select and then improve system robustness.

GD³ is a comprehensive strategy to help prevent and eliminate problems (see Figure 4.4). GD³ starts with a design that most closely achieves the needs and desires of the customer and the organization. This can be accomplished by either creating a new design or reusing an existing design. Efforts are then taken to find the hidden buds of problems through discussion of the issues generated at the interfaces between parts and systems. (*Buds of problems* are unseen issues that exist in a design that unfortunately may bloom later when your product is in

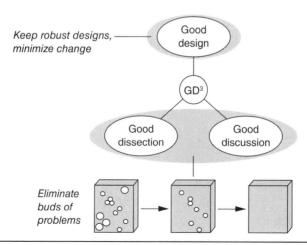

Figure 4.4   GD³ diagram.

production.) Finally, buds of problems are found by testing the product and evaluating changes in physical properties that may create a problem if the design was tested longer or harder.

The first step in generating a good design is to establish an initial good or robust design. For this step, two options are available: (1) reuse a robust system or (2) create a robust system. The preferred solution for good design is the selection of a system that is already robust (see Figure 4.5). There is far less risk in reusing a robust system than in creating one. The downside of reuse, however, is that the ultimate potential may be limited. If robust systems are unavailable, or if the most robust system does not have a high enough performance potential, a system may have to be created. When creating a robust system, care must be taken to use the best DFSS tools to create a system that is robust to known control and noise factors. At the same time, you must understand that the major risk of creation is the effect of unknown and unknowable interactions. Minimizing the effect of these unknowns is accomplished with good discussion and good dissection.

An analogy for robust design could be the creation of a winning baseball team. You could hire ball players who have a high batting average, or you could take the gamble of hiring lesser known players through the draft. The veteran player may have a high batting average but be very expensive, unable to hit

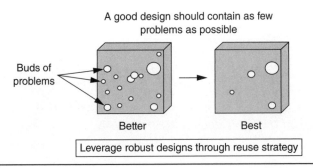

Figure 4.5 Good design.

certain pitches, or unable to improve above his current level of play. The new player found in the draft is more of an unknown but might have the potential for an even higher batting average at a considerably lower salary.

Extensive work must be done to create robust systems; therefore, it may be more desirable to obtain robustness by reusing less robust systems. Improving less robust systems is accomplished by minimizing change, finding and correcting problems, and eliminating unseen buds of problems that may exist within the design. These unforeseen problems can have disastrous consequences on a new launch. The bloom of these buds typically smells like stinkweed, not roses.

All designs will have buds of problems. The strategy is to find the design with the fewest number of problems and then eliminate them.

Eliminating these buds of problems requires good discussion and good dissection. Good discussion is the comprehensive review, with a collaborative team, of all design changes, especially those changes at the interface between different parts or systems. All designs (even the most robust) contain buds of problems. Unfortunately, almost all designs require some tweaking or redesign before they can be used in the final product. These design or process changes (even those meant to improve the quality of the design) create additional buds of problems. Finding the buds of these problems must be accomplished prior to the part or system going into production. These buds of problems are found in two locations: in the components themselves or at the interface between the components.

By the nature of most product design, engineers are assigned to create or modify individual parts. Multitudes of parts are then brought together to form a system. Rarely are engineers assigned to the interfaces between parts (see Figure 4.6). This space is the responsibility of the two individuals whose parts share a common boundary. Unfortunately, this discussion and partnering rarely occur.

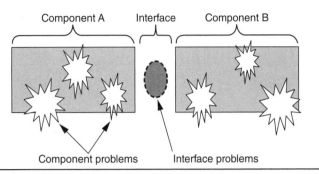

Figure 4.6   Location of problems in immature systems.

For companies early in their quality journeys, most problems occur in the individual parts or components. As engineers and designers learn from their failures and drive robustness into their designs, the number of component problems falls and the remaining problems occur at the interfaces between parts (see Figure 4.7).

To find the buds of problems in the initial design, most companies use DFMEA and PFMEA (design and process failure modes and effects analysis). D/PFMEA is essential and required. Unfortunately, it is usually written early in the design stage and rarely updated, even when the component or system is used in different applications. To eliminate the buds of problems, an additional step is required: a DRBFM.

The specific purpose of the DRBFM is to find and correct concerns based on changes in the design with special attention at the interfaces of the component with other systems. The DRBFM format, shown in Figure 4.8, is a combination of a design failure analysis with a group technical discussion (usually called a peer review). This review is centered on changes to the design and the possible consequences of these changes.

A good DRBFM (1) focuses on changes in the design and the surrounding conditions or environment, (2) is used to facilitate good discussion to identify buds and define countermeasures, and (3) if done correctly, can identify more

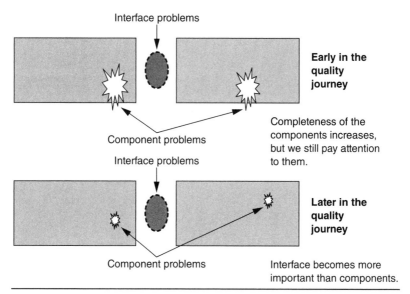

Figure 4.7   Location of problems in mature systems.

Part name/ part change or effect of changed environment	Function of the part	Points of concern related to the change	Cause of failure mode/concern		Effect on customer		Design actions to eliminate concerns (provide details and best practices used)	Recommended actions (results of review)					
		Any other concern (review)	Cause of failure mode/ concern	Any other cause (review)	On customer or system	Severity		Design to include	Response/ target	Evaluation to include	Response/ completion date	Production to include	Response/ target
D	D	D	D		D		D						
			R	R	R	R	R		R	R	R	R	R	R
			(combines DFMEAs and peer reviews)										

Figure 4.8   DRBFM.

invisible problems (buds) than hardware testing and identify them earlier.

The second stage of the process to find and eliminate the buds of problems is called good dissection. Good dissection is completed during validation testing. After all failures have been identified and documented for correction, a team reevaluates the components and systems for other changes that were not reported as failures. The purpose is to look for changes in physical properties. Although these changes in properties did not produce a failure, we must ask whether these changes could signify an early indication of a future failure if additional cycles were completed or environmental conditions were different.

An ideal and complete validation plan could be visualized by the ability to color-in the box (see Figure 4.9). Current validation practices (as represented by localized dots) do a relatively poor job in completing that task. (This is not the result of incompetence of your validation engineering staff but the hard facts associated with gaining statistical confidence.) If at the same time, for every validation test, the physical properties were evaluated for change and those changes reviewed, discussed, and corrected as required, validation could more closely color-in the complete box. In other words, buds of problems that would have entered through production into the field would have been comprehended and eliminated prior to production.

A good design review based on test results (DRBTR) is successfully completed by (1) looking at all parts for changes in physical properties that may provide additional clues to buds of problems, (2) increasing your knowledge by dissecting test samples, and (3) analyzing the test methods and results to understand the design weaknesses.

A key part of both the DRBFM and DRBTR processes is *Genchi and Genbutsu*, which is Japanese for "go and see in the field or test location." Good designs, discussions, and

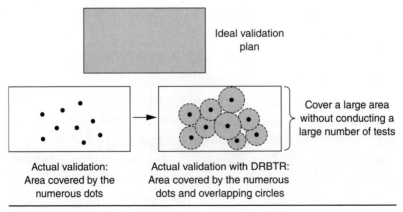

Figure 4.9   Good dissection.

dissections *cannot* occur without hardware, parts, and physical properties being evaluated at the location where the failures occurred or the designs were tested. GD^3 is a key driver in your APAT strategy.

The second APAT discipline is *Interface with your downstream customer*. We often treat our downstream customer as a separate and different entity. The downstream customer must accept whatever we give them. Figure 4.10 illustrates how planning dumps on design, design dumps on validation, validation dumps back on design, design dumps on production, and finally production dumps on the customer. You have to ask yourself whether this is the ideal development process and whether it really puts the customer first.

The best products are developed with great cooperation with your downstream customers and upstream suppliers. Cooperation is not demanding that the requirements you have established be met by those downstream; it is going both upstream and downstream and working together to create a great system (see Figure 4.11).

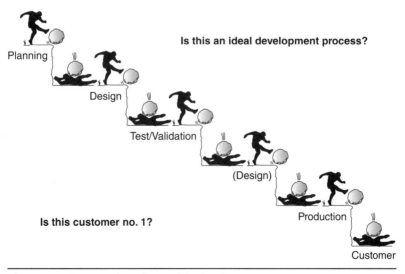

Figure 4.10 Poor interface with the downstream customer.

Source: Adapted from an illustration by Tatsuhiko Yoshimura.

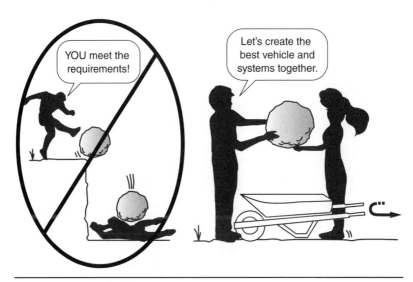

Figure 4.11 Creating the best product through teamwork with APAT.
Source: Adapted from an illustration by Tatsuhiko Yoshimura.

I was once part of a team of automotive engineers who were challenged with coming up with the best engine noise containment package. The team researched the technical and university journals and came up with a system that was significantly better than the competition. The team dove into making production drawings for its new and radical concept. Throughout the development process the production engineer on the team kept saying that the design could not be built in the assembly plants. Although the engineers heard the concerns, they thought the production engineers were just complaining and looking for the easiest way for the plant to produce the product. The day came to assemble the noise control system into a preproduction vehicle, and lo and behold, the production engineer was right: The system could not be built. With this newfound reality of buildability, the team rapidly diverted back to the old system of noise control. Unfortunately the space required for the sound deadening material had already been given away for other uses. A final correction was established that weighed more, was more costly, and did not perform any better than the competition's system.

Work with your suppliers, manufacturers, and assemblers. They, along with your customers, all have great ideas that will support the success of the product. Remember that the success of the process is measured not by who was right but by how satisfied the customer feels.

The third APAT discipline, *Change management*, builds on the GD^3 process. All change creates opportunities for buds of problems to enter into robust designs. Often these buds are created at the interface between robust systems, sometimes blooming into stinkweed. Minimize change, eliminate buds of problems, and review and discuss all changes with your downstream customers.

One of the most tragic examples of a bud blooming into a problem is the Kansas City Hyatt walkway collapse in 1981. The original design called for two suspended walkways being supported by three pairs of threaded rods. This design had a considerable factor of safety. In the construction phase a small change was made to aid in the building of the hotel (does this sound like anything in your business?). Instead of running the three pairs of threaded rods all the way from the ceiling to the lowest level, the design was changed so that the upper rods held only the upper walkway and additional, shorter rods were used to connect the upper walkway with the lower walkway (see Figure 4.12).

This change in the assembly of the walkway seemed small and of minimal effect, but the consequences were significant. At a dance contest in 1981, when approximately 2000 people were in the atrium, the small change (the small bud) resulted in a major disaster. The total load on the upper walkway connection was too great and the joint failed, which resulted in both walkways crashing down onto the crowd below. A total of 114 people were killed. Although this is an extreme case of a bud of a problem blooming, we often add buds to our designs and processes

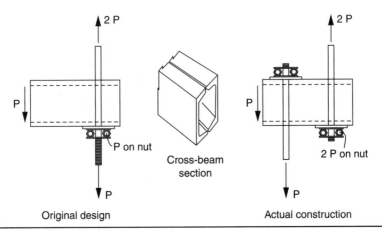

Figure 4.12   Kansas City Hyatt walkway design.

daily. We must review every change, even if it is small; we must also ask whether the changes could add any unforeseen buds that could produce new and different failures. Look for events where changes frequently enter into your design and development process. Changing designs for cost reduction or quality improvement adds buds. Moving from prototype to production tools adds buds. Moving from prototype to product processing and locations adds buds. Be very cautious of the no-brainers or the minimum changes; sometimes these generate the biggest stink.

A second example shows the result of nonrobust engineering followed by buds of problems growing into a catastrophic event. The de Havilland Comet was the first commercial jet airliner in the world. The Comet first flew in 1949 and was considered a benchmark for British aviation. Soon after introduction, however, a number of early aircraft suffered severe metal fatigue that resulted in catastrophic failure and subsequent great loss of life. After several crashes and multiple groundings, a complete root cause analysis was completed. Its finding was that aircraft structure failure was the result of stress concentrations, a consequence of the square window shape (you never see a square window on aircraft today). Several problem buds also existed. The aircraft engineers knew that square windows would produce some stress concentrations and had required all windows to be drill riveted and glued. But in production, the windows had only been punch riveted. These two buds (punch riveting and no glue), coupled with the square window stress concentrations, were enough to cause a catastrophic and near-instantaneous metal failure as the airliners were at cruising altitude. Buds of problems are even more critical when designs lack significant amounts of robustness, but in even the most robust designs you must be conscious of any bud of a problem being introduced.

The net result was that the Comet had to be redesigned, but the damage was already done. By the time the new Comet was designed and produced, American manufacturers Boeing and McDonald Douglas had caught up with their own jetliners (707 and DC-8, respectively). Later models enjoyed long and productive usage, but sales never recovered from earlier enthusiasm for the Comet.[1]

The fourth APAT discipline is *Teamwork*. To win requires the engagement of the entire workforce. We all believe we are great at driving teamwork.

Unfortunately, the desire to get extremely specific on job assignments drives workers to concentrate on their own assignment and to be less concerned with those jobs around them. I would theorize that although we all know about teamwork and have demonstrated teamwork in our lives, we rarely actually live teamwork.

Let's look at an easy example. We all learned to play baseball when we were youngsters. Remember playing on defense? When the ball was hit toward the first baseman, everyone ran

---

[1] Report of the Public Inquiry into the causes and circumstances of the accident which occurred on 10 January 1954, to the Comet aircraft G-ALYP, Part IX (d). http://www.oocities.com/capecanaveral/lab/8803/fcogalyp. htm#galyp.

toward first base. The second baseman ran toward first base, the pitcher ran toward first base, and the outfielder ran in toward first base. Why? Isn't it the first baseman's job to field the ball? Of course it is. But it is everyone's responsibility to back up and support the first baseman. Winning is not measured by the players playing only their position to the best of their ability. Winning is about the team leaving the field with more runs scored than the opposing team. All of us can name great sports teams. In some cases those teams were led by a few great players, but in most cases we struggle to identify individuals because the team was made up of many good (not great) players who worked together.

Teamwork is about getting with your upstream and downstream partners. It's about knowing what is required for your customers and providing it. It's about communicating with your upstream suppliers and supporting them in delivering what you need to be successful. Teamwork is not only about playing your position to the very best, but also about knowing the position played by your teammates and supporting them when they run into difficulties. Remember, winning this race is not about the cumulative results of each individual but the cumulative results of the total team. Figure 4.13 shows the two different philosophies of team play. Team A requires each team member to specialize in their position and not worry about other positions around them. Team B requires each player to not only play their best but also support the players around them. Which team do you think has teamwork?

The fifth APAT discipline is *100/100*, which means 100% of the results requires 100% participation. To be the best, 100% of your workforce must be engaged 100% of the time. Even though it makes great business sense to get 80% of the effort with 20% of the resources, it is not good enough to get just 80% when your competitor is driving 100%. Everyone in engineering, manufacturing, and purchasing must act and behave as though they are personally responsible for their sys-

Figure 4.13 Which is teamwork?

tems. They must all drive to make sure their systems are satisfying their customer's needs and not failing.

The discipline 100/100 requires personal knowledge from
the field on the performance of your system and a personal
commitment to making it better. People who are 100/100 are
constantly scouring the internet looking for complaints. These
are the people you usually see late at night analyzing the information to learn and improve their parts and systems. Engineers
must make sure their parts and systems are designed and developed with great quality. They make sure they spend whatever
time is required to make their systems robust. Suppliers and
purchasing must make sure that every part purchased adds to
this greatness. It is not about parts meeting prints; it's about
parts making great systems. Marketing must make sure that
every customer call, every dealer visit is of high quality.

The sixth APAT discipline is *Continuous improvement*. It is
the responsibility of every individual to look for opportunities

to improve the design or process. Many companies have groups responsible for reviewing customer data to determine what problems should or should not be worked on. This process does two things: First, it insulates the engineer from the customer, and second, it allows some engineers to not be responsible for their systems. Every engineer must take full responsibility for the parts and systems he or she designs. If those systems or parts are not great, every engineer is personally responsible for getting involved in identifying and solving problems.

One significant constraint to any quality improvement process is the required financial funding. Most funding is provided by an equation that tries to balance engineering and production expenses with the cost of warranty. The typical question asked is, what is the warranty cost comparison versus the cost of the improvement? If the warranty cost is more than the cost of the correction, the obvious decision is made to correct the problem. But if the cost of the repair is more than the warranty, then much soul-searching and leadership are required to correct the problem. The difficulty in justifying the corrective action is reduced by looking at all of the quality costs, both internal and external. Additional external costs may include lost future sales, rebates, or any additional costs of advertising and marketing due to poor quality. Additional internal costs are the costs of inspection and containment. These additional internal and external costs typically do not make the business school ledger and are often difficult to apply.

The situation becomes even more difficult if the failure is outside the normal warranty period, such as many wear-out or durability issues. Driving continuous improvement of durability issues poses unique problems compounded by two factors: (1) the quality problem occurs outside the warranty period and therefore does not have any direct warranty cost, and (2) durability problems usually follow an exponential failure rate. This exponential growth rate means that small frequency durability failures will typically grow significantly as products age. You often see only the tip of the iceberg of the quality problem. If you wait until the failure rate grows enough to see the evidence, you will have years of production in the field (the best time to kill the monster is when it is young; if you wait too long, the monster may kill you).

The best quality companies go beyond the argument of "should we or shouldn't we correct a quality problem?" A strategy I learned from Tatsuhiko Yoshimura is called "anti-aging." The philosophy of anti-aging is simple: As soon as you see the failure, introduce the correction. Do not wait for the failure to grow; do not wait for the business model to catch up. Implementing the anti-aging process requires great leadership, but the rewards are product leadership in quality and reduced cost later associated with recalls and product rebates.

The seventh and final APAT discipline is *Eliminating waste and adding value*. All processes contain waste; we must be diligent in eliminating it and making sure all processes add value. Any activity that does not improve a part or a process is waste. Any process that involves only checking and reporting is waste. After all activities we must ask, "Was the product improved?" If the product was not improved, look for ways to add value. One such method is by identifying weaknesses and eliminating possible problems. A computer aided engineering (CAE) group I worked with provides an excellent example. The CAE group was required to evaluate vehicle structural strength for ride performance, durability, and crash protection. If the strength was not sufficient, additional structure was recommended (value was added). But if the strength was sufficient, no additional analysis was completed (no value was added). After seeing that in the second case no value was added, this group took a leadership position in adding value and changed the paradigm so that if the strength was sufficient, further analysis was performed to reduce the mass and/or cost of the system.

Following these seven disciplines of APAT will greatly drive your quality performance well beyond that of focus strategies.

APAT strategies can and should be applied by everyone in your organization.

Typical quality literature identifies the quality journey as beginning with a Pareto. Although I have always been a believer in the Pareto principle, I have come to understand that the Pareto by itself is *not* sufficient to command quality leadership. The Pareto usually drives the philosophy of getting 80% of the value for 20% of the effort. The 80/20 principle is a fantastic place to begin your quality journey, but it is insufficient to win. To win, you must drive for 100% of the value with 100% of the effort.

APAT strategies require that all of your workforce be working on quality, not just a selected group or individuals. The attributes of APAT strategies are as follows: (1) Everyone is engaged, all the time, (2) tools are simple and easy to use, (3) ordinary people have the ability to be successful, (4) time is very effectively managed, and (5) teams and groups are recognized as heroes and rewarded.

Focus and APAT strategies can be extremely complementary on your quality journey. To demonstrate the need for both, let's review the quality of two similar products—in this case, two vehicles in the same luxury class. Figure 4.14 shows the results of a questionnaire sent to the customers of two competing products. Around 130 questions were asked, and the frequencies of issues reported are tracked on the vertical axis.

There are several similarities between the two vehicles. First, both products reported quality problems. Second, both have a well-defined-problem Pareto. There are also some significant differences between the two vehicles. From looking at the Paretos, it is obvious that Vehicle 2 has higher quality than Vehicle 1. If a team applied some focus-strategy problem solving to Vehicle 1, they could improve the quality nearly to the level of Vehicle 2.

Working on only the largest problems will not allow Vehicle 1 to achieve the same quality. Looking at the far right side of

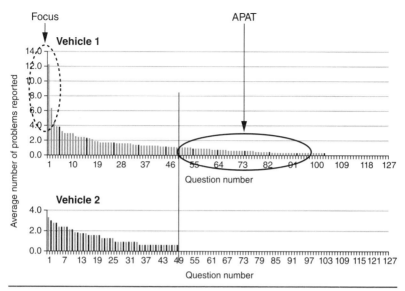

Figure 4.14 Focus strategy vs. APAT strategy.

the Pareto, we can see that customers did not report any issues on a large number of questions. Many infrequent problems occur in Vehicle 1 that do not show up in Vehicle 2. Applying only focus strategies will not address these problems. To achieve this quality level requires some APAT problem-solving strategies. In this case, I am familiar with both teams and know that the team working on Vehicle 2 drove both focus and APAT strategies.

For discussion, let's say the top problem was reported at a frequency of 12, the second at 5, the third at 5, the fourth at 4, and the fifth at 4 for a total of 30 problems. If a concerted effort was applied to these problems and a 50% reduction was achieved (50% would be very significant), the total number of problems would be reduced by 15. At the same time, let's look at the right side of the Pareto graph. There are approximately 40 questions that have less than 1 reported problem, for an average of ½ problem per question. If these issues were eliminated, the total product quality would improve 20 problems. In conclusion, the total quality of any product is not only about the frequency of the most significant issues but also about the accumulative effect of issues that occur infrequently.

Every opportunity to prevent or eliminate any problem should be taken. Winning requires not just the lowest failure rate of your biggest problems but also the lowest number of problems, period. Although I agree that a Pareto provides a good list of problems with which to start your quality journey, if all you follow are focus strategies, you will have little advantage over your competition. To win, you will have to drive APAT strategies as well as focus strategies.

The Pareto should be used to provide insight into what gets worked first as well as where the top resources and best tools should be directed. Although this seems sound and reasonable, the Pareto, unfortunately, often allows the rest of your organization to become disengaged. To be the best, your entire organization must be on the same quality journey with the same enthusiasm. Everyone must be working on his or her own quality improvement plan. It is not the responsibility of only a handful of key individuals or engineers in your organization to carry the whole load of quality improvement; it is the responsibility of everyone in the organization, if you truly plan on winning.

Although the APAT name may be unfamiliar and the strategies foreign, if you look around your company you will find a number of APAT strategies already in place. You may have a corporate United Way fund drive or a blood drive. Both of these are APAT strategies. A great example of such a situation was one Fortune 500 company that stated it did not have any active APAT strategies in place. Under review, this company learned that it was not the best in employee safety. Its accident rate was about 20 times the very best company rates. The drive to be the best in employee safety became an overriding goal of the company. To reach that goal, two initiatives were started. First, all known incidents were identified and eliminated. A Pareto of the known incidents was established, and teams were created that methodically eliminated these known problems. This is a perfect example of a focus strategy. Second, all *possible* incidents were eliminated. Any situation that could cause an injury, such as tripping over electrical cords or cutting your finger when slicing a bagel, was eliminated. This is a perfect example of an APAT strategy. Following these two strategies, the company was able to achieve its desired safety goal within a few years. It had been following an APAT strategy without having knowledge of APAT.

Although you must apply both focus strategies and APAT strategies to win the quality race, there will be times when you may want to move initiatives from focus to APAT or the reverse. A great example of moving from focus to APAT is in the broad use of the statistical engineering strategy. Many tools in statistical engineering can and should be done by all people, such as solution verification or paired comparison. In *solution verification* you apply your solution to several occurrences of the problem to confirm that you are able to turn the problem on and off. In *paired comparison* you review several pairs of good/bad parts or systems to look for contrasts between the two. Many tools that begin as focus tools are easily taught to "all the people."

Going from APAT to focus strategy is a little more difficult but still possible. The method to move from APAT to focus is called *concentration*. Concentration provides the ability to recognize patterns and opportunities in data that often seem random or dispersed. I have found that there are two types of concentration: natural and derived. *Natural* concentrations occur without any outside influence. Some examples of natural concentration are high air-conditioning failures in vehicles in Phoenix, Arizona, and high cell phone failures in teenage users. In both cases, failures may not be recognized when looking at all customers in North America but are easily detected and corrected when looking at concentrations due to environment or customer usage.

Derived concentrations occur because of outside influence. Some examples of derived concentration include performing all warranty work in a handful of locations (as near to the engineering facility as possible) or concentrating production of specific products as close to the market as possible. Customer clinics as well as product shows (electronics or autos) are additional examples of derived concentration. In these examples, warranty repair, production, and market research can be optimized for effectiveness and efficiency by concentrating through management direction. Within quality I have found many natural and derived concentrations (see Table 4.1).

Concentration is often used in a breakthrough discussion (more on breakthrough in Part IV) to generate ideas for rapid

Table 4.1   Concentration types.

Concentration	Detail	Type
Failure mode	Concentration of failure modes	Natural
Failure phenomena	Concentration of common customer concern notification	Derived
Problem-solving resources	Concentration of problem-solving engineers and technicians	Derived
Infant system failure	Concentration of systems (assembled parts)	Natural
Infant part failure	Concentration of young parts	Natural
Excitations	Concentration of excitation conditions	Natural
Environments	Concentration of environmental conditions	Natural
Regional	Concentration of common global failures	Natural
Warranty repair	Concentration of returned parts	Derived
Quality clinics	Concentration of select customers	Derived

growth in your quality plan. Concentrations can provide clues to new and creative strategies to significantly improve your quality processes. Concentration allows us to drive the engagement advantage of the APAT thought process into the speed and effectiveness of a focus thought process.

Let's review some natural examples of concentration. Failures within a system almost always follow Pareto distributions (I have never seen an example of a failure mode that didn't). For each failure there is a primary, secondary, and tertiary cause. Since failure causes add by the square root of the sum of the squares, the largest cause is significantly more important than the second largest cause, and the same for the third and fourth causes. Knowledge of this fact leads to rapid elimination of a failure through the elimination of only the largest causes. This is the principle behind statistical engineering (or Red X) problem solving. A second example is environmental conditions. There are always some areas of the country that are significantly colder, hotter, wetter, or saltier than other regions. These differences always produce concentrations. If you want to see the largest concentration of vehicle air-conditioning failures, go to Phoenix in August. If you want to find the largest concentration of home furnace problems, go to Calgary. Likewise, there is solar exposure, humidity, salt, or corrosive environments. Look at which environment is the most stressful on your parts and then look for areas of the country that experience that environment.

Different loading and usages can also be natural concentrations. If you want a lot of vehicle failures, then look at taxi or mail fleets. Similarly, cell phones get the most abuse from teenage users. For global companies, some countries may have larger failure rates than others. It is amazing that the same product never produces the same failure rate in each country. Parts and systems can also be natural concentrations. If you have specific infant mortality issues with certain parts or assemblies, the part concentration may be more easily seen at the supplier or assembler.

Derived concentrations can be established by management. Problem-solving resources can be a derived concentration. One company had three different groups working on the same failure mode. Each group was fighting over the same failed parts and the same key test fixtures. In such a case, bring all the problem-solving groups together, and bring the failed parts to them. Warranty repair can also be concentrated. If you have warranty work done at many locations, concentration can occur by doing warranty work at only a handful of locations or possibly only one location. Typically, fleet and returning lease vehicle warranty work is handled at each dealership, spread throughout the country. If instead you can concentrate warranty work into a handful of dealers close to problem solvers, you can increase your problem identification and correction efficiency. A marketing clinic may also be used as a derived concentration technique. Marketing people have used clinics for many years to concentrate customers. You can do the same with customer satisfaction. Pick a location with a significant number of customers and invite them to talk or bring in their products to be serviced or repaired. Finally, customer notification can also be used as a derived concentration strategy. In the present world of vehicle telematics and internet notifications, modifications can be made to improve notification and recognition of failure concentrations.

In each of the upcoming chapters on the Five Cs, I will attempt to identify both focus strategies and APAT strategies. As you read and think through the processes, I am sure you will come up with your own initiatives.

> *Driving APAT strategies can provide sustained quality improvements. Tools and problem solvers can be directed at the large number of very small problems and results obtained early in the design and development cycle. Driving APAT*

strategies can provide long-term assurance that you will close the quality gap with your competitor. APAT strategies will initially be unnatural and awkward to implement. Cultural changes will be required to fully implement the strategies. Ultimately, the combination of focus and APAT strategies can provide you the ability to beat your competitor in quality.

ADDITIONAL READING

Chowdhury, S. 2005. *The Ice Cream Maker: An Inspiring Tale about Making Quality the Key Ingredient in Everything You Do.* New York: Doubleday.

Yoshimura, T. 2002. *Toyota Style Mizenboushi (Preventative Measures) Method—GD³: How to Prevent a Problem Before It Occurs.* [In Japanese.] Tokyo: JUSE Press.

PART III

Quality Structure— The Five Cs

Care
Contain
Control
Correct
Create

All the
People,
All the Time

5

The Five Cs of Quality

This chapter discusses and reviews the five key categories of
quality formation. A short outline of each category describes
the value, ownership, and timing of each grouping and how
the five make up a comprehensive quality strategy.

Quality initiatives and tools can be broken down into
what I call the Five Cs of quality: create, correct, control, contain, and care. These five categories of initiatives are differentiated by the amount of improvement that can be
achieved, the speed in which the improvement can be obtained,
and the organization most responsible for their implementation.

Like the pyramids of old, the Five Cs are constructed so that
their strength is based on the foundation. The foundation spreads
the load of the whole pyramid over a wide area. Each progressive level requires a much smaller area. In the Five Cs, the base
is "create." If sufficient effort is made in creating robust products, less time will be spent on correction, less time on control,
less time in contain, and at the top of the pyramid, less time in
special care and apologizing to your customers (see Figure 5.1).

Let's start with the foundation of our quality pyramid: create. Create (or creation) involves the process of establishing
or building-in design and/or process robustness. ASQ defines
robustness as "the condition of a product or process design that
remains relatively stable, with a minimum of variation, even

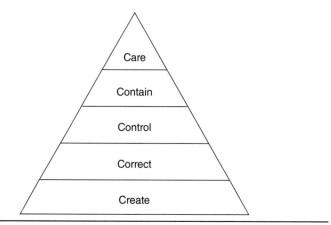

Figure 5.1 The Five Cs.

though factors that influence operations or usage, such as environment and wear, are constantly changing." *Robustness* is the characteristic of a design where its performance or function is insensitive to variations in build, assembly, usage, environment, or time.

If your products are not created with robustness, the strength and stability of the whole quality plan are jeopardized. Create is followed by the additional layers of correct, control, and contain, and finally capped by care. Not only is care the pinnacle, it is often the most visible and personal aspect of your quality plan with your customers.

Continuing the pyramid analogy for your quality plan, all levels of the pyramid are not built simultaneously. The foundation is built first and covers the largest area. Each succeeding layer is built on top of the previous layer. For any product, the process is the same: First you style or design the product, and then you engineer it. This is followed by testing and improving the product, starting production on the product, and finally, controlling production of the product. Lastly, you sell and service the product.

In Figure 5.2 I have identified the magnitude of quality that can be obtained by each step and the length of time that is

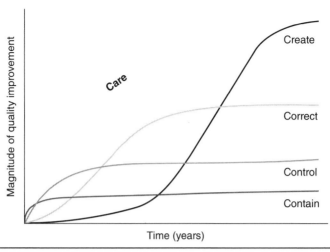

Figure 5.2 Magnitude of quality achieved by the Five Cs.

required to achieve that improvement. Care does not have a specific curve or improvement rate but involves correct behavior when issues arise in any of the quality improvement categories. From this chart you can see that creation takes the longest time to implement but provides the greatest improvement, followed by correct and control. The last category, containment, can be almost immediate but provides the least amount of improvement. Let's look briefly at each of the five categories in reverse order.

Care is the intense focus on immediate solutions to a customer's needs that enhance the customer's experience with your product. Care is making things right in the customer's eyes. It is being accountable and having integrity even when there is no legal obligation to do so. Some of the tools available within care are customer communication, executive customer contact, extended warranties, owner loyalty recognition and certificates, product exchange, reimbursement for expenses, and support for repurchase. Care is the only category of initiatives that is not included as a curve in Figure 5.2. Care is an attitude. Care is about consideration and assiduousness for your products today. At the same time, care is not just about the final customer. Within any product development process there are many handoffs. Each handoff has a supplier and a customer. Your immediate customer may be the engineer or supplier right beside you. Make sure you care for the next operator on the line or the next engineer in the process, just as you would care for the final customer.

Contain is the insulation of your customers from product deficiencies until irreversible corrective actions can be accomplished. Containment is taking charge of your future today. It is taking immediate action at any location that is producing defects. Containment is about not building or shipping any product that does not meet your expectations. Some of the tools in containment are quality reviews and gates, on-line inspection stations, third-party inspection, and shipping holds. In Figure 5.2, containment shows almost immediate improvement followed by marginal or no improvement. The list of issues to be contained are quickly identified and addressed, but the list does not grow very rapidly. Although improvement is rapid and essential, the value is limited. An unfortunate consequence of containment is the additional expense of adding manpower or equipment to contain the product. Make sure that with every containment process implemented you also initiate a control or correction project to eliminate the containment initiative and its associated costs.

Control is the continuous improvement in the stability and capability of both products and processes. Many call this process variation reduction. Many quality professionals split control issues into common and special cause contributors, and then concentrate on special cause concerns. But control is more than just managing special cause concerns. It is about the systematic elimination of the possibility for defects to be created. It is about kaizen, error proofing (poka-yoke), and living FMEAs. Some of the tools in control are control charting, precontrol, layered audits, error proofing, living FMEAs, and product audits. Control produces more improvement than containment but requires more time to get started (see Figure 5.2). Additional time is required to find the opportunities and start the process of eliminating special cause issues and reducing common cause issues. Like containment, control produces fairly quick improvement followed by continued but reduced improvements. Although the costs of control are less than the costs of containment, they may still be significant, primarily due to the cost of manpower. Again, for every control process initiated, it is often worthwhile to initiate a correction process to eliminate the control.

Correct is about aggressive problem solving. Correction is about finding the one or two contributors to any problem and modifying them to eliminate that failure mode. It may involve changing a process or a product attribute to ensure no defects are produced. Some of the tools in correction are statistical engineering (Shainin Problem Solving), problem solving, 5 Whys, Kepner-Tregoe, engineering change, and product improvements. Correction is often called firefighting. Expert problem solving is a highly desired commodity in any organization, and many careers have been made by problem solving. It can be one of the most rewarding jobs in a company. Problem solving usually takes more time to initiate because of the skills required to do it well. Problem solving has the ability to produce considerable gains. The drawback for correction is that it is typically started or accelerated in production, which means that tools and processes must be modified or changed. These modifications can add considerable investment costs to your product as well as add complexity to your service parts operation.

Create is the final category of quality initiatives and the most significant. Create, or creation, is about robustness. It is about the process of making new designs that are insensitive to environmental variation and customer differences. It is also about making designs that are insensitive to both build and manufacturing variation. Some of the tools in creation are DFSS, Taguchi methods, DOE, robustness assessment, axiomatic design, and engineering change. Creation or design robustness takes the longest time to implement. It essentially requires a component or system to be created, re-created, or reengineered. Creation has the largest potential to maximize quality. One additional benefit of creation is that unlike its four partners in quality strategies, it can be implemented alone without relying on customers to report field failures.

Dr. Joseph Juran described the quality journey in a model that has been affectionately called the Juran Trilogy. The trilogy represents the demonstrated quality of a product through the complete design and development cycle. I use the word "demonstrated" to reflect that the quality is measured from physical hardware. Over time the quality improves because problems are continually being found and corrected and because the hardware is continually evolving into the production parts being manufactured by production processes. In the trilogy the vertical axis is the quality level and the horizontal axis is time. There are several key points to the trilogy. The first is identified in Figure 5.3 as a circle (near time zero), representing the quality of the initial design produced by prototype tools. This point, as well as the downward curve on its right, is identified as a period of creating, or development robustness—area 1 in Figure 5.3.

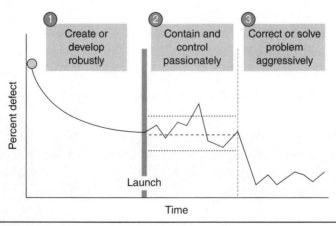

Figure 5.3 Juran Trilogy quality model.

Area 2 is identified as the period of manufacturing, where quality improvement is obtained by process containment and control. Area 3 is the period of correction or product improvement.

The graph is divided into two sections by the launch line. Up to the launch line, the quality plan is completely contained within your company. After the launch event, your quality plan will also involve your customer. Our Five Cs fit nicely within the Juran Trilogy.

Creation or robust design begins years before a new product enters production. It is during this time period that the inherent quality is designed into your product. The circle on the far left in Figure 5.3 is identified as the initial design robustness. This is the cumulative robustness of all the parts and processes that make up the final product, as well as the interaction between the parts and processes. The initial design robustness is established through your design and engineering process and is influenced by the amount of carryover robustness of parts and processes as well as the created robustness of new systems and parts. Both carryover robustness and new part robustness are influenced by DFSS and other quality tools. Once the product is designed, prototyping and validation testing begin. Your testing and validation have the potential, as well as the responsibility, to identify nonrobust systems and improve them. As problems are found and corrected, the quality of the product improves, as shown by the descending line. I call this the *glide path*. A rigorous plan can be made that identifies the probable glide path of your product development. As product hardware is made and tested, you can track the test results on the glide path and modify the quality plan to change your improvement rate to achieve the desired glide path. At the point of launch, the product must be at the predetermined quality on the glide path to meet your customer's expectations.

At launch, everyone must be engaged with the manufacturing and assembly plant to find and correct any problems not previously caught. When your first product is transported to your customer, the customer becomes engaged in your product improvement plan, which most of your customers do not want to be part of. Customers do not want to be involved in product failures, missed expectations, returned product, and procuring new product. Your customers never want to be your durability tester. Therefore, you must take every action to launch flawlessly. A flawless launch implies a launch without quality or timing incidents. Remember that your launch products are also the products that magazines will purchase, test, and write about. Make sure these early products meet your expectations.

Following launch, normal production begins. Although I call it "normal production," it is anything but normal. Everyday production is a battle: a battle to control the hundreds and thousands of processes within your plant, as well as monitor the quality of hundreds of suppliers that are also trying to maintain control. During this battle you are trying to run at 100% of your rated capacity while trying to improve the quality of your product. Although most manufacturing plants have occasional hiccups, they are able to maintain fairly consistent production and quality.

To maintain production, most plants rely on a combination of containment and control. Everyday feedback comes from internal indicators as well as from the field. This information provides details on which processes need improving or have drifted out of control. If the information identifies a process out of control and the process can be monitored, then inspection and sorting should be initiated immediately. If the process tends to drift or vary over time, then control methods should be initiated. Although containment and control are essential and required, they require manpower and time, with only limited prospect for improving quality or productivity long term.

Although Figure 5.3 shows the control and correction processes as separate stages, they actually occur at the same time and one often leads to the other. Systems that run out of control require problem solving, and all good problem solving ends with control. For additional information, I suggest *Juran's Quality Handbook*, in which Dr. Juran spends considerable time outlining control and correction.

Containment and control make up what I call "strategies to not get worse." Often the best that can be hoped for in driving these strategies is for the process to remain the same. If your strategies are only containment and control, you will probably see some initial and quick improvements followed by slow deterioration in the output of your processes, even with extra effort. To change the game, you must drive "strategies to get better," which will point you back up to create and correct. These two strategies provide lasting improvement with minimum cost.

> *The five key categories of quality formation are create, correct, control, contain, and care. Together, they provide the means to create a solid pyramid of quality attainment. Implementation will provide a means of obtaining almost immediate improvement, followed by a long-term strategy to accelerate the quality drive.*

ADDITIONAL READING

Juran, J. M., and J. Defeo. 2010. *Juran's Quality Handbook: The Complete Guide to Performance Excellence.* 6th edition. New York: McGraw Hill Professional.

Mizuno, S. 1992. *Management for Quality Improvement: The 7 New QC Tools.* New York: Productivity Press.

Taguchi, G., S. Chowdhury, and Y. Wu. 2004. *Taguchi's Quality Engineering Handbook.* New York: Wiley Interscience.

6

Care

Care

This chapter discusses and reviews the care category of quality formation. A brief definition of care is provided as well as some of the author's experiences. Included in the chapter are both focus and APAT strategies you can implement to start your own care program.

*C*are is the intense focus on immediate solutions to customer needs that enhance the product ownership experience. Nothing turns me off from a product faster than it not living up to my expectations. The other thing that turns me off is a company that does not understand my concerns or honor a commitment to my satisfaction.

I have owned a multitude of products that have prematurely failed or have never quite lived up to the expectations advertised. In most cases, the manufacturer was *not* open to any discussion of replacing the product or reimbursing some of my expenses. I have never given these companies a second chance for my business.

Care for the customer is by far the most emotional (both good and bad) quality initiative a company makes. Since satisfaction of your customer is a key strategy for getting into and staying in business, caring for the customer is of prime importance.

It often amazes me that a company that has no problem offering significant rebates to capture a customer will struggle with the concept of spending a few dollars to keep a customer. A good example of this was told to me by a service technician from a large company. One of his long-term customers was experiencing a problem with one of his products, and it was just outside the warranty period. Because the product was technically outside of warranty, the company would not reimburse any customer expenses. This customer owned many thousands of dollars worth of this company's most expensive product and probably would continue to be a valuable customer in the future. But because of a failure a few days outside of warranty and the lack of a few dollars in someone's budget, this customer was lost forever.

Conquesting a customer provides no assurance that the individual will remain a customer forever. Likewise, there are no guarantees that a long-time customer will remain loyal. The rebate that is offered today to coax a customer to your product may only make it necessary to "buy" that customer again tomorrow. On the other side of the coin, some "special care" that is provided to a customer today will be remembered and appreciated well into the future.

Several years ago the vice president of quality for an automotive company asked me to contact several customers who had contacted him. Those first few customer phone calls led to a passion of mine to try to call one or two customers every night on my hour-long trip home from work (it also added to the APAT notion of adding value; the trip home now had value to my employer). My list of potential contacts came from a supply of disgruntled customers who had written about the poor experience they had with the product my company produced (when your company makes thousands or millions of a certain product, you will get letters).

As I continued to work with customers, the purpose of the call changed. At first, my desire was to appease my boss. That desire changed to a passion to transform poor customer experiences into great experiences. I changed my goal from just getting through a couple of calls a day to asking for letters and setting a goal of plastering my office with the many thank-you cards I received from the customers I helped. My goal was to keep loyal 95% of all the customers I called. I am proud to say that I achieved that goal. I then added a second goal: For every disgruntled customer I called, I would attempt to contact either a friend or a relative of the original customer. My list of satisfied customers is lengthy, from the customer in northern Michigan who sends me a jar of thimbleberry jam, to the customer in Tennessee who sends me a Christmas card every year, to the customer who sends me encouragement notes and pictures from California. Each of these customers has become part of the family, and I hope that none of them ever leave my product. Loyalty often cost me only a few dollars and several hours of listening and understanding.

The best way to satisfy a customer in the long term is to make sure the product performs the same on the last day of ownership as it does on the first day of ownership. Unfortunately, the laws of physics cannot be violated, and your product *will* deteriorate. To win, your product must hold its value *longer* than your competitors' products do. It must also not deteriorate faster than your customer's expectations, which may be driven by experiences with your competitor. Some random failures may occur. If they do, they must not inconvenience your customer.

The ultimate strategy is to eliminate your failures (the other four Cs discuss the elimination of failures). Quality improvement takes time, and therefore you may have customers who are dissatisfied with poor-quality products manufactured some time ago. Some manufacturers have implemented care programs by extending their warranty for a longer time period; this is a good first step. Although this will reduce the cost to your customer, it does not relieve the customer of the inconvenience of having to return the product to a warranty center. In addition, many manufacturers cannot afford the cost of a warranty extension. If your company is one of them, there are some more affordable options: gradual extension of the warranty period, warranty proration, or co-pays. You will find that most of your customers are reasonable and understanding. You need to reach them at that understanding level. Protecting your customers from excessive expenses is a good place to begin. It is also beneficial to add a personal contact if possible, to make sure the customer is heard.

As I stated earlier, it became my goal to contact one or two disgruntled customers every day. This is a great focus strategy that should be applied on a larger basis. I initiate my calls on the basis of the letters received. This strategy could be expanded into an APAT strategy and made proactive. Figure 6.1 shows a typical warranty analysis of a complex product. On the vertical axis are the percentages of customers who report problems. On the horizontal axis are the numbers of problems reported.

For this product, about 50% of the customers reported absolutely no problems or product concerns. About 88% had fewer than 2 problems, but a handful of customers reported as many as 15 problems. You may suspect that this manufacturer

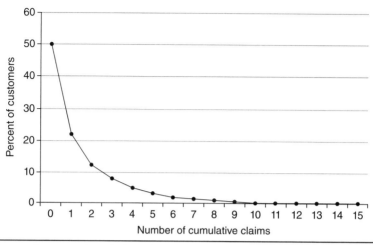

Figure 6.1 Product failure claim distribution.

produced poor quality, but actually this manufacturer is one of the best in quality. Even this world-class producer had some customers with expectations that were not achieved or products that failed more frequently.

The question is, what will you do for those customers reporting a large number of problems or dislikes? If you do nothing, they will more than likely leave for your competitor. Although losing a few customers may seem inconsequential, you must remember that these customers may tell hundreds of potential customers about their concerns and your lack of appreciation for their problems. These potential customers, who are now informed, rightly or wrongly, may refuse to shop your brand.

You need to activate a program to contact these customers immediately. You might argue that they have unreasonable or unwarranted expectations. I have called hundreds of customers, and some will try to take advantage of you, but this is extremely rare. Most customers are at the opposite end: They hate to bother you but appreciate the opportunity to talk. After playing phone tag with some customers, I gave up and gave them my home phone number (sales and service almost always discourages this because of the fear that the customer will call constantly). These customers almost never called me at home, and when I asked why, they said they did not want to bother me. Can you believe it? These customers had many concerns and they did not want to bother me. All manufacturers have a number of customers with significant issues with their product. Start with these customers; they are probably leaving because of poor quality and lack of attention.

Now that you have identified them, how do you contact them? Be cautious of letting just anyone contact your customers. Treat your customers as a delicate and perishable commodity. The use of entry-level employees or contract employees should be discouraged. Although these employees can be and usually are well intentioned, they do not have the insight into the problems the customers are experiencing, nor do they have the clout to reimburse or provide remediation to the customer. An even worse thing is to have these entry-level employees tell your customers that they work for the president or the chairman. Inadvertently, some customer will ask for something that does not meet your contacting employee guidelines. The customer will be disillusioned because he or she knows that the president or chairman of a company would surely have great latitude in providing support. By this action, your credibility and that of your employees will be compromised.

A second fault I find with many customer contact processes is the final step of arbitration or lawsuits. Although a process must be in place for the unreasonable customer, too often the process recommends litigation much too quickly and too easily. Lawsuits always end up in a double loss. By double loss I mean that if your customer wins the lawsuit, you lose, and if you win the lawsuit, you still lose the customer. This does not sound very good to me, since you lose both ways. Instead of quickly moving to a lawsuit, find your best customer contact and give this person some additional tools and processes to keep the customer. To show true acceptance of the desire to care for your customers, have the president or chairman of your company call a handful of customers each year.

Some of the actions that can be taken when you call customers are the following: reimbursement of expenses, warranty extensions, buy-back of the product, certificates reducing the price on new products, elimination of payments, or maintenance packages. Although buying back a product is rarely required, an interesting touch is to put the products that are bought back into the hands of your employees. I know a car company that would occasionally buy back vehicles and put them in the company fleets so that the employees could experience what the customer was experiencing.

Now let's talk about APAT strategies. APAT strategies can include things you do for all customers or things that all of your employees can do to support your quality. Let's look first at what can be done for all of your customers. An example is from a purchase I made about 10 years ago. I had purchased an expensive product, and about three weeks after the purchase I received a flashlight and map in the mail. These gifts were totally unexpected. It felt like Christmas in June and significantly increased my loyalty to this company. Gifts to your customers do not have to be expensive, but they do have to work. The worst thing you can do is to give a gift that fails prematurely. *Do not* send cheap gifts that fail; this will not only add cost but will actually reduce loyalty. It is better not to attempt this type of APAT strategy than to attempt it and have it backfire. Another APAT strategy for your customers can be an extended warranty, or at least an extended warranty with a percentage covered by a deductible. As much as your customers hate returning a product for warranty work, they hate it even more when they have to pay a large sum to get the product repaired.

Several years ago I participated in a pick-up truck clinic in Dallas, Texas. This was an unusual clinic in that we did not have the customers look at new vehicles; instead, the manufacturer invited only customers with vehicles over 40,000 miles (all vehicles were outside of warranty). The customers were then asked to list all of their problems with their vehicle. The customers' vehicles were then repaired free of charge. The comments from the customers were phenomenal. Most could not believe that any company would provide that level of attention to someone who had not bought one of its products for so many years.

Look at getting all your employees engaged. Many companies allow employees to give away their employee discounts on new products. This could be extended for vehicle repair. Some have suggested each employee adopting four or five customers. Each employee would be given a limited budget to spend per month on repairing customers' products. Be creative; ask for suggestions from your employees. Think about the products you buy: How did you feel when they did not meet your expectations? What would you have wanted or required to maintain your loyalty?

A great example of gaining customer loyalty is Discount Tire. I had taken three tires (none of which were purchased from Discount Tire) in to be repaired—two had nails and one had a rim leak. I expected to pay for the repairs and was surprised to hear, "No charge, but please consider us the next time you buy new tires." Obviously Discount Tire understands that its profits are generated by selling new tires, not repairing tires, and one way to get loyal customers is to provide tire repairs for free (even on another company's tires). Last year I bought $800 worth of new tires from Discount Tire.

During my many customer calls I have received much wisdom from the customers. One particular customer told me he felt like a snowflake: small and having little effect or impact. At the same time, he said that enough snowflakes can make a glacier, and glaciers can move mountains. Moving mountains can be beneficial or objectionable. Work with your customers. They have the ability to make you rich or put you out of business.

The care you show your customers should also be translated into your product development process. In this case the customer may be the engineer or designer who sits next to you or down the hall. If your action causes him or her distress, then make it right; put the extra effort into fixing the situation. Also remember that the production facility is your downstream customer. Care for your downstream customers in your development process the same way you care for your external customers.

I have been told that you lose customers one at a time and that you need to regain them one at a time. Make the appropriate changes to move this from a slogan to reality.

> *Care is the overall encompassing strategy of direct intervention in the resolution of customer concerns. This category of quality strategies contains the actions that you must take because of poor quality so you can live to fight another day. An enthusiastic care process can allow you to earn another hearing from your customers. Care is about treating your customers the way that you would want to be treated. Care is about listening, caring, compassion, and intervention. It is about going the extra mile and showing the customer that he or she means something to you and has value. Do not be known by the rigidity of your rules, but by your humanity and passion for your customers.*

ADDITIONAL READING

Sewell, C., and P. B. Brown. 2002. *Customers for Life: How to Turn That One-Time Buyer into a Lifetime Customer.* New York: Currency.

7

Contain

Contain

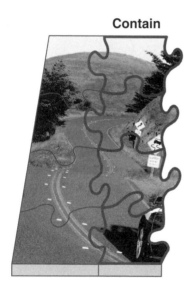

This chapter discusses and reviews the contain category of quality formation. A brief definition of contain is provided as well as some of the author's experiences. Included in the chapter are both focus and APAT strategies you can implement to start your own containment program.

One of the most immediate actions you can take in your quality journey is to stop the flow of defective products to your customers. *Contain*, or containment, is the insulation of the customer from deficiencies until irreversible

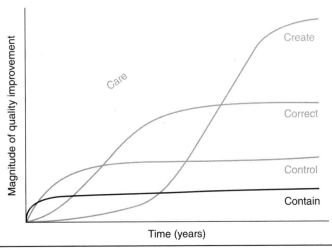

Figure 7.1 Contain—one of the Five Cs.

corrective action can be obtained. Containment is the *most immediate* quality process outlined in Figure 7.1.

When a defect is found, immediate steps should be taken to alert someone of the issue and stop the cause of the problem. If a part is being installed incorrectly, or if parts are out of specifications, you must take quick action to stop the flow of defects.

Although containment brings immediate improvement, long-term improvement is limited. This is because containment tends to lose its effectiveness over time. An additional drawback is that for many defects, no containable action will be found.

Over the many years I have been in quality and quality engineering, I have visited numerous manufacturing and assembly plants. Four plants stood out as having greater quality than the others. One automotive instrument panel plant in Brazil had the most error proofing (poka-yoke) of any plant I had ever seen. Every operation had some means of error proofing, and at the end of several processes additional error proofing occurred. A second automotive assembly plant, in Oshawa, Ontario, Canada, had an extremely large and experienced group of problem solvers. These individuals could quickly identify the root causes of any problems that came up and correct them.

The third plant, an automotive transmission plant in Windsor, Ontario, Canada, had the best containment and control logic I had ever seen. PFMEA became living documents that directed newer and better containment and control logics. The last plant was an automotive assembly plant in Kentucky. It had very active control processes and a very good understanding of active containment strategies. One thing each of these plants had in common was the rapid containment of issues followed up by extensive control and problem solving.

All containment begins with the identification of an issue. Therefore, for containment to be active, information from the field and from within the plant must be quick, detailed, and assignable. The identification of issues is the catalyst that starts the containment initiatives and thus stops the flow of defects to the customer.

Although all industries and services could and should use containment, the food and medical industries have used containment the most aggressively. As food and medical quality often drive life-or-death consequences, rapid and swift containment is mandated. A good, but at the same time unfortunate, example of quick containment was in a hepatitis outbreak in Michigan in 1997. In March of that year, an outbreak of about 150 cases of hepatitis A occurred in Calhoun County. Information was quickly routed from the local health services to the Centers for Disease Control (CDC) and the United States Department of Agriculture (USDA). Investigators quickly learned that the outbreak was caused by contaminated strawberries served in school lunches. The strawberries were traced back to a processing plant in San Diego that also shipped strawberries to schools in five other states. In this containment initiative, all strawberries were recalled and a hepatitis immunization program started for the potentially affected students in all six states. The outbreak was quickly contained with no additional occurrences of disease. Although the true root cause was never determined (Americans pointed to unsanitary conditions in the Mexican strawberry fields, and Mexicans pointed to unsanitary conditions in American packing and distribution plants), control methods were set up to monitor sanitary conditions in both the American processing plant and the Mexican strawberry fields. An additional change was that the USDA now requires the packing date, lot number, and country of origin on all frozen foods. This will allow complete root cause analysis of any outbreak in the future.

As I stated, there is always a cost associated with containment. Many companies complained vigorously about the cost and difficulties associated with new USDA packaging and tracking guidelines. In addition, since the root cause was never determined, strawberry farmers in both California and Mexico suffered the consequences. The remaining strawberry crops that year went to waste, as no produce distributors wanted to take the risk of purchasing tainted product.[1]

A second example of containment was in the Tylenol recall of 1982. On September 29, 1982, Mary Kellerman of Illinois died after taking a capsule of Extra Strength Tylenol. Adam Janus, also of Illinois, died shortly thereafter. Adam's brother and sister-in-law died after gathering to mourn his death. Investigators soon discovered the Tylenol link and started the containment process. Urgent warnings were broadcast, and police drove through Chicago neighborhoods issuing a warning over loudspeakers.[2] Johnson & Johnson, the parent company responsible for Tylenol, distributed warnings to hospitals and distributors and halted Tylenol production and advertising.

The person responsible for the contamination was never caught. In November 1982, Tylenol reintroduced capsules but in a new, triple-sealed package, coupled with heavy price pro-

[1] CDC, "Hepatitis A Associated with Consumption of Frozen Strawberries—Michigan, March 1997," http://www.cdc.gov/mmwr/preview/mmwrhtml/00047129.htm.
[2] Rachael Bell, "The Tylenol Terrorist," Crime Library, truTV.com, http://www.trutv.com/library/crime/terrorists_spies/terrorists/tylenol_murders/index.html.

motions. The tragedy prompted the pharmaceutical industry to move away from capsules, which were easy to contaminate because a foreign substance could be placed inside without obvious signs of tampering. Within the year, the Food and Drug Administration (FDA) introduced more stringent regulations to avoid product tampering.

The medical industry has taken containment to an even higher level. The FDA and the Consumer Product Safety Commission classify recalls into three classes:

- Class 1—involves a health hazard situation where there is a reasonable probability that the use of the product will cause serious health consequences or death

- Class 2—involves a potential health hazard situation where there is a remote probability of adverse health consequences

- Class 3—involves a situation where the use of the product is not likely to cause adverse health consequences[3]

As in the food industry, containment in the medical industry is rapid and complete and often begins with information from the field. It is often started after an adverse condition within the public (sickness or death) becomes present. Although sickness and death may not be the consequences of poor control in your business, you should have an attitude of containing the problem just as the food and medical industries do.

Just as there are examples of good containment, there are also examples of poor containment. Several automotive manufacturers have been accused of producing vehicles that have unintended acceleration, such as some Toyota models in the early to mid 2000s. By 2009 over 2000 complaints had been identified, and 89 people were reported to have been killed by vehicles suddenly accelerating without driver input. In an

---

[3] FDA, "Background and Definitions," http://www.fda.gov/Safety/Recalls/ucm165546.htm.

example of a poor containment process, Toyota, normally associated with high quality, first attempted to blame some of the acceleration on customers, who may have accidentally—or even intentionally, as reported in the *Los Angeles Times*[4]— pressed the accelerator pedal instead of the brake (although drivers sometimes do press on the accelerator instead of the brake, a quick check of other vehicles would have revealed an unexplained higher incident rate). When complaints continued, Toyota initiated a recall of floor mats, which the auto manufacturer believed got bunched up when the accelerator pedal was pressed. Again complaints continued, so Toyota initiated a recall of gas pedals, which the auto manufacturer believed became nonresponsive over years of wear. The true root cause, however, may have been something other than the floor mats or the accelerator pedals. In an NPR broadcast of March 9, 2010, host Michele Norris interviewed *Los Angeles Times* business reporter Ken Bensinger who stated that in some cases unintended acceleration continued even after the floor mats were replaced and the accelerator pedals were repaired.[5, 6] Data from State Farm Insurance support the reports that unintended acceleration in Toyota Camrys more than tripled after the automaker introduced electronic throttle controls. In addition, top Toyota executives testified to Congress that they were not sure whether the problem had been solved.[7]

[4] Ralph Vartabedian and Ken Bensinger, "Runaway Toyota Cases Ignored," *Los Angeles Times*, November 8, 2009, http://articles.latimes.com/2009/nov/08/business/fi-toyota-recall8.
[5] Ken Bensinger, "Examining Toyota's Acceleration Problem," interview by Michele Norris, *All Things Considered,* March 9, 2010, http://www.npr.org/templates/story/story.php?storyId=124501322.
[6] Ken Bensinger and Ralph Vartabedian, "Data Point to Toyota's Throttles, Not Floor Mats," *Los Angeles Times*, November 29, 2009, http://articles.latimes.com/2009/nov/29/business/la-fi-toyota-throttle29-2009nov29.
[7] *U.S. News and World Report*, "Toyota Owners Encounter Acceleration Problem after Recall Fix," March 4, 2010, http://usnews.rankingsandreviews.com/cars-trucks/daily-news/100304-Toyota-Owners-Encounter-Acceleration-Problems-After-Recall-Fix.

Several lessons may be learned from these containment exercises: If you have a problem, (1) do not blame it on your customers (take responsibility for it quickly), (2) monitor the field and quickly start a containment if needed (delays only increase the size of the problem), and (3) get to the true root cause as quickly as possible, using outside resources if necessary (you should never have to initiate multiple recalls for the same concern).

Product issues can be identified from numerous plant process inspection stations, the final plant audit, or from the field. When an inspection or review of a product identifies a defect, notification must be made immediately. In an assembly plant, notification is commonly done by an andon cord signal. An *andon cord* is a cord that runs the length of an operation and is attached to an alarm that sounds when an operator detects an issue and pulls the cord to signal that extra effort must be made to stop the defects immediately. Typically the process is twofold. The first pull requires a team leader to respond to fix the issue. If a second pull, signaling that the defect has been fixed, does not occur within a given time, the line shuts down so that the defect does not pass to the next station.

I once visited a plant that had just installed andon cords, and the senior managers were complaining that the cords did not work; their operators would not pull the cords for any defect. The managers interpreted the cords not being pulled as a lack of quality concern among their employees. Occasionally I find employees who do not care, but it is very rare. For a whole plant to not care is unthinkable. For this reason I stuck around for a few days to see what would happen. Sure enough, at the end of the first day, several defects were found in audit. I took these failures back to the respective department to find out whether the defect was identified in the build station and why the andon cord had not been pulled. What I found was that each area did have an andon cord, the employees understood the process of pulling the cord, and they had even seen the defect. When I asked why they had not pulled the cord, they all stated that when the cord was pulled, a 98-dB alarm went off and some manager came running down the aisle asking who the jerk was who pulled the cord. After a few name-calling incidents, they decided it was easier not to pull the cord and to let the defects flow. As I will discuss in the last chapter (on success), management has the ability to both nurture and throttle success.

Different forms of containment are 100% inspection, third-party inspection, and reinstructing the operator. Remember the old adage that 100% inspection is only 80% effective? No containment is 100% effective. Effectiveness over time may deteriorate due to operator rotation or operators creating shortcuts.

As described in the chapter on GD^3, don't forget to contain the interfaces. There are many interfaces in any plant. At most plants, workers begin when the line starts. A critical interface is between the two or three shifts of workers. I always wondered how effective job instruction training is if you're struggling to keep up with the line. Who determines what was completed in the last shift and what needs to be done on the next shift? The interface in this instance is between shifts: what was completed on the night shift versus that which needs to be completed on the day shift. From my experience, at the end of the shift, workers are eager to leave the plant and may leave some jobs incomplete. Likewise, workers on the next shift often do not get to their respective job locations until the line actually begins. This leaves little time for any inspection of the previous shift's final products. The solution to this problem could be as easy as providing some time prior to line start for operators to walk up the line and inspect the last products of the previous shift.

The following solutions help ensure that critical operations have trained operators: (1) Start critical operations 15 minutes early so that operators have time to train in a less hectic time period, and (2) limit the number of critical operations within a supervisor or team leader's area so that the trainer can be full time on a critical operation. The absolute best containment is to have highly trained operators building systems in a consistent manner.

Looking at the Juran quality model (Figure 7.2), we can see that containment is one of the key drivers in stabilizing the quality at the old quality level and kicking off the system to a new and improved quality level.

There are numerous APAT strategies that should be implemented for containment. It must be communicated that it is everyone's responsibility to not pass on any defect to downstream operations. Everyone should look at the next operation as his or her customer. To make sure no defect is passed on, every operator must know exacting details on the quality expectations for his or her operation. Special care is needed between shifts or after any job rotation or substitution. Every shift must make sure that all operations were completed from the previous shift. Some of the best manufacturers have detailed descriptions of each operation as well as detailed definitions of the quality standards. No operator is certified for any job unless he or she performs the job exactly as described and has complete knowledge of the quality standards.

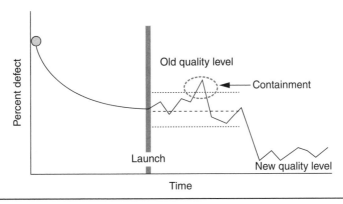

Figure 7.2 Quality model—containment.

If the quality standards for any job are not known, you must go downstream and ask those operators what is required to be complete and the level of quality that is expected. Continue with each operation until each job is defined and each operator knows his or her individual level of quality to attain.

> *Contain, or containment, is the insulation of the customer from deficiencies until irreversible corrective action can be obtained. Contain is a key part of any quality strategy. It is the most immediate of any of the strategies and must be rapidly and enthusiastically used to stop the flow of defects to your customers.*

8

Control

Control

This chapter discusses and reviews the control category of quality formation. A brief definition of control is provided as well as some of the author's experiences. Included in the chapter are both focus and APAT strategies you can implement to start your own control program.

*C*ontrol is the continuous improvement in the stability and capability of product and processes. After containment, the next quickest quality improvement strategy is control, as shown in Figure 8.1. Containment and control make

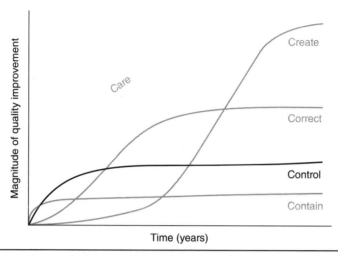

Figure 8.1   Control—one of the Five Cs.

up the twin sisters of manufacturing quality. The use of control strategies will bring about quality improvements by identifying and eliminating special (versus common) cause variation. Special cause is typically associated with manpower or process-induced variation such as operator training and tooling.

Control can be broken down into tool control, process (manpower) control, and supplier control. Some people might add engineering control to the list, but I will not, although engineering can certainly get out of control. Control can also be broken down into active or passive control. Control is focused on maintaining consistency and reducing variation.

I often see manufacturers asking for an engineering change when any problem is detected. If a manufacturing plant has been running without defects and a defect is found (and no engineering changes were made), the root cause of the defect lies within the manufacturing or supplier walls, not in engineering. With the proper problem-solving process and skilled problem solvers, the root cause should be found. Engineering should be used only if the corrective action is too expensive, is too time consuming, or is not able to ensure long-term quality.

Be cautious of engineering's willingness to support problem elimination with engineering changes. Engineering is almost always willing to make changes and takes great pride in the ability to improve products. At the same time, all engineering takes time, costs money, and could produce buds of problems that lead to additional problems. Engineering should be brought in only if it is used to support problem solving or if corrective action cannot be determined within the plant or supplier facilities.

If engineering changes were made prior to manufacturing problems being detected, then engineering may be the cause of the problem. It may be advisable to review the process or parts before the change and determine whether reverting back will eliminate the issue.

Many companies maintain continuous improvement processes that can have anywhere from 5 to 18 steps. I am most fond of a six-step problem-solving process. Figure 8.2, showing the six-step process, is a standardized way to look at solving any problem that may occur in production. The first three steps involve control; the last three steps involve correction (problem solving).

The six steps work best when issues are discovered within a manufacturing process, but they are also applicable for issues discovered in the field (in the hands of your customers).

The six steps begin with the detection of a problem. If the problem is found in the manufacturing plant, you begin with the first question. If the problem is found in the field, you need to look at the clues before determining which step to begin with (described later in this chapter).

The first three steps describe typical special cause problems. That is, the process has been running without incident (under control) until a problem occurs. Question one is the first step in identifying the discrepancy. It asks, "Is the correct process being utilized?"

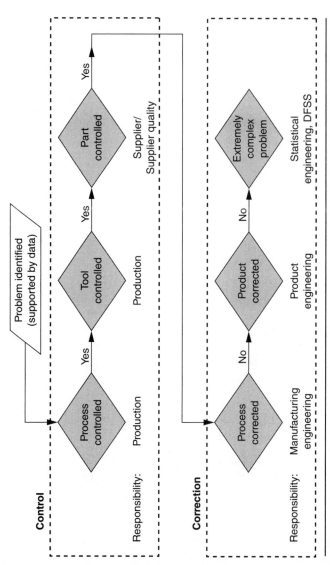

Figure 8.2   Standardized problem solving.

Depending on the type of discrepancy, the following audit questions may be asked about process control:

- Has the standard work for the job been identified?

- Are the correct standardized work sheets posted?

- Is the standardized work sheet being followed?

- Are the correct supporting documents posted at the operation?

- Is the job being performed to the product assembly standards?

- Has a mandatory sequence been identified? Is it being followed?

- Is the job being done the same way on both shifts?

- Does the operator understand what the product quality standards are?

- Has there been operator turnover on the job?

- Has the operator been properly trained?

- Are the visual aids current?

- Does the operator understand the quality outcomes of her or his job?

- Does the operator know how to communicate when there is a problem?

If all applicable audit questions are asked and the source of the discrepancy has not been uncovered, then proceed to the second step.

Inquiries during step two are intended to identify problems related to production tooling. Question two asks, "Are the correct tools being utilized?" Depending on the discrepancy, the following audit questions may be asked about tooling control:

- Have the standard tools and fixtures been identified?

- Are the correct tools and fixtures being used?

- Are the tools set to the specified torque?

- Are the tools properly calibrated?

- Are both shifts using the same tool?

- Are the bits or sockets worn?

- Has an extra air hose been attached to the tool?

- Is the tool tied to the andon cord system?

- Has the tool been put on bypass?

- Do the tools and fixtures have mutilation protection?

- Are appropriate error-proofing techniques used?

- Does the workstation layout allow the operator to work effectively?

- Has preventive maintenance been done?

- Are tools functioning correctly?

If all applicable audit questions are asked and the source of the discrepancy has still not been uncovered, then proceed to the third step.

Step three determines whether the parts specified in the product assembly documents are being utilized. It asks, "Are the correct parts being utilized?" Depending on the discrepancy, the following audit questions may be asked about parts control:

- Have the correct parts for the operation been identified?

- Are the correct parts on the job location?

- Is the part routing current?

- Are the correct part numbers identified on the material racks?

- Are parts stocked in the correct location on the rack?

- Do the part numbers on the boxes agree with the rack?

- Are all andon pull cards available (andon pull cards are for the proper distribution of parts)?

- Has engineering changed part usage?

- Is error proofing needed?

- Is the existing error-proofing device working correctly?

If all applicable audit questions are asked and the source of the discrepancy has still not been uncovered, then escalate step three to your suppliers. This escalation raises the question of part quality to your suppliers. It asks, "Has the part quality changed?" Notice that the question does not ask, "Are the parts meeting the specification?" Having the parts meet the intended quality specification is a very appropriate question if the specifications have been statistically generated or if new production is just starting. Specifications are typically "historically" generated and are "tuned in" during early production until quality assemblies can be produced.

The plant quality control team reviews the parts to ensure they meet overall part quality. If the part quality is suspect, the team needs to:

- Set up sorting operations to provide good parts for the operation

- Work with group leaders to validate countermeasures or containment

- Notify the supplier that a problem has been detected and that its parts are suspect

- Send 3–5 pairs of good and bad parts to the supplier for analysis and ask the supplier to follow the first two problem-solving steps (see the appendix for paired comparison logic)

- Work with supplier quality to validate the corrections

If the data reveal that part variation is within established part specification but is still producing suspect assemblies, then engineering should:

- Work with the supplier and supplier quality to adjust the part specification range

- Work with the plant engineering team to determine whether an engineering change is required to provide irreversible corrective action

If the root cause of the problem cannot be found in the first three steps of the problem-solving model, then proceed to step four, process correction.

Historically, the main method for maintaining control has been control charts. More recently, businesses have been moving to precontrol charting. Although I used control charts extensively earlier in my career, I have grown less and less fond of them over time. I have seen many occurrences where processes were building outside of specifications (requirements), but due to the control chart averaging process, poor-quality parts were not contained. On a regular control chart, samples are taken, averaged, and plotted. Usually this takes place at the end of the day, so production of poor-quality parts could have occurred all day. Alarms may have been raised because of measurements near the control limit, but the seriousness of the situation was not detected. I have become more enthusiastic about precontrol charts for numerous reasons: (1) They are easily understood (green is go, yellow is caution, and red is stop), (2) neither multiple samples nor mathematical computations are required once the control limits (performance variation) are established, and (3) actions can start immediately. Once a measurement is taken and plotted on the precontrol chart, you know immediately if you should go, stop, or take an additional measurement.

Many of the best companies for quality have taken the additional step of error proofing, or what may be called active control. In this case the control is active or built right into the operation. An example of active control is in torque control. Instead of just monitoring torque, torque is read on each usage of a tool. If the proper torque is not applied, the line will not advance to the next operation. Another example is in the presence or absence of locks or pins. In this case, the specific number required is released, so if the operator has one left when the job is finished, then he or she knows that one lock or connector was not completed. Many books have been published on error proofing or poka-yoke, and many of them contain examples for every industry.

The APAT strategies for control are complementary to those for containment. Each operator must have complete knowledge of the process to complete the job. The parts that are required for each model must be presented to the operator in such a manner that it is impossible to use the wrong part in the assembly. Error proofing for every process, no matter how simple, is a great APAT control goal. In addition, the quality expectations for each operation must be clearly communicated and understood. The quality expectations may be supplemented with minimal quality checks, such as a tug on an electrical connector or the visual inspection of color on an identification tag. The testing may also be more extensive, such as providing full power application to an electrical circuit.

To provide additional control, boundary samples, part specimens, or pictures must be available for all operations so that all parts or processes can be quickly evaluated against the quality standard. If parts are not readily available, again go downstream and look for parts that have been pulled from systems and been rejected. If none can be found in the manufacturing plant, continue looking in the field (remember that failures in the field are due to failed parts or failed systems).

Some of the best and worst examples of control are in the chemical and nuclear industries. Chemicals must be mixed to very exacting quantities, so any deviation can produce disastrous consequences. Great control produces a continuous flow of products with no news headlines. Poor control disrupts this continuous flow and can produce very negative news headlines. According to many accounts, the Bhopal Union Carbide incident is an example of the some of the poorest control in history. On the night of December 23, 1984, a dangerous chemical reaction occurred when a large amount of water got into a methyl isocyanate tank. Almost 40 tons of methyl isocyanate escaped the plant, and nearly 4000 people were killed. The root cause of the accident revealed that gauges measuring temperature and pressure (two essential control parameters) were so unreliable that workers ignored early signs of trouble. In addition, refrigerating units and gas scrubbers were shut off or not working.[1]

Nobody talks about the thousands of chemical and nuclear plants that run flawlessly every day due to rigid control procedures and error proofing. It is the handful of plants that do not follow rigid control or have not spent the time on error proofing that provide negative publicity for the entire industry.

> *Control is the continuous improvement in the stability and capability of product and processes. Control is a key part of any quality strategy. It is the second most immediate of any of the strategies and must be rapidly and enthusiastically implemented to stop the flow of defects to your customers.*

[1] "Bhopal Disaster," TED Case Studies, http://www1.american.edu/TED/bhopal.htm.

ADDITIONAL READING

Ishikawa, K. 1982. *Guide to Quality Control*. White Plains, NY: Unipub/Quality Resources.

———. 1985. *What Is Total Quality Control?: The Japanese Way*. Englewood Cliffs, NJ: Prentice Hall.

———. 1990. *Introduction to Quality Control*. New York: Productivity Press.

Juran, J. M., and J. Defeo. 2010. *Juran's Quality Handbook: The Complete Guide to Performance Excellence*. 6th edition. New York: McGraw Hill Professional.

Mizuno, S. 1988. *Company-Wide Total Quality Control*. Tokyo: Asian Productivity Organization.

9

Correct

Correct

This chapter discusses and reviews the correct category of quality formation. A brief definition of correct is provided as well as some of the author's experiences. Included in the chapter are both focus and APAT strategies you can implement to start your own correction program.

C ontain and control are primarily about making sure a product does not drift from a given quality level. They are also used to prevent possible failures due to manufacturing and assembly variations. Be cautious: Although containment and control can lead to rapid improvements in quality, both improvement rates can stagnate over time. Dependence on containment and control can lead to an emphasis on "strategies to not get worse." If a company concentrates only on these strategies, the best it can hope for is that things do not get worse. Reliance on these strategies may result in your actually getting worse. A "strategy to not get worse" must be complemented with a "strategy to get better."

Also called problem solving or firefighting, *correct* (or correction) is about the permanent elimination of existing problems. Correction can lead to great product quality improvement. Correction is the first initiative where sustained and significant improvements can be achieved (see Figure 9.1). Correction is about reducing failure rates, not just controlling them.

For many companies, "firefighting" and "firefighters" are revered. Many current executives can attribute their promotions to their ability to kill problems. Although correction can produce great improvements in product quality, the benefits of problem solving take time. This time constraint is due to the length of time required to train problem solvers, identify prob-

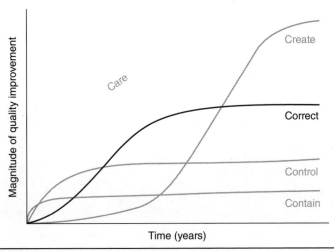

Figure 9.1 Correct—one of the Five Cs.

lems, determine the root cause, and establish corrective actions. Correction is the first step in moving to a significantly different (better) quality level. In the Juran quality model (Figure 9.2), correction is the fuel for the transition of a part or system to a new quality level.

There are five important facts you should know before you start your problem-solving journey. First, *you probably make great product every day, but not all of it is great.* For this reason you must leverage the differences between your good product and your bad product. Do you know what makes the good ones good and the bad ones bad? The question that must be asked is, why do the same parts and processes allow some products to be good and some to be poor? Your very best products are called BOBs (best of the best), and your very worst products are called WOWs (worst of the worst).

Second, *most of your individual problems can be solved by making one change*, sometimes two, and at most three. These changes may be a torque, a dimension, an assembly sequence, or a part of material property. Numerous changes are not required to solve most of the problems you experience. As a matter of fact, if you do make a large number of changes, you will more than likely cause the product to deteriorate in quality.

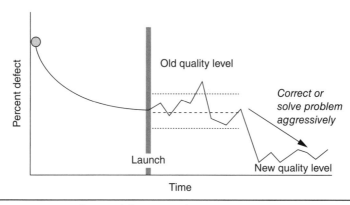

Figure 9.2 Quality model—correction.

Third, *you do not have to solve thousands of problems to make a significant improvement in quality.* Usually, just solving a few problems (or hundreds of problems if your product is very complex and contains thousands of individual parts) can significantly improve your product. To begin problem solving, you should generate a Pareto of your problems and issues (focus strategy) to identify the areas of largest opportunity. At the same time, to be the absolute best, you will also have to employ some APAT strategies. Unfortunately, although many quality improvement plans contain many focus strategies, very few contain APAT strategies.

Fourth, *some problems are easily solved, while others require advanced problem-solving support.* For this reason you must have an escalating problem-solving process with ever-increasing levels of capability and expertise. You will need to form a group of problem solvers who are capable of solving even the most difficult problems.

The fifth and final rule is that *today's significant issues* (I like to call them "hardy perennials") *will also be tomorrow's significant issues unless you understand the physics, correct the problem, and transfer the lessons and knowledge into the future.* Hardy perennials are your most difficult problems. They are like weeds: They show up not only in your yard but in your neighbor's yard (your competitor probably has some of the same problems). It does not matter how many times you cut them down; they keep coming back. To eliminate hardy perennials, you must have special problem-solving and prevention skills to get to the true root of the problem.

Most people feel problem solving is straightforward and not very technical. This is only the case when your quality is poor and you have a large number of problems to solve. As your quality level improves, your problem solving becomes more difficult. For complex products (such as vehicles, electronics, or appliances), the current best quality level may be near one problem per unit sold. Although this may seem large, remember there are hundreds (if not thousands) of individual systems that make up the product. Fortunately, many failures have minor significance. For less complex products, the current quality level will be significantly less than one failure per unit sold. To get a better understanding of the nature of product failures, let's dissect the complex product that has less than one issue per product (one issue includes both failures and dislikes). Many people believe that the number of unique problems will be relatively small, but that is not the case. Figure 9.3 is a typical distribution of failures for the family of products that average one issue per product.

To achieve a quality level of one issue per product, the problems coming from your customers will be wide and varied, with only a handful of issues being over 1% in frequency and the majority being less than 0.1% in frequency. The first significant block of problems will be those between 0.49% and 0.2% in frequency. Keep in mind that a 0.2% failure rate implies that 99.8% did not fail. Attempting to fix a 0.2% failure rate could result in changes that do not fix the problem or, worse, generate new failures with rates larger than 0.2%.

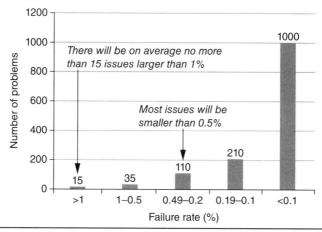

Figure 9.3 Average of one problem per system: issue distribution.

A second concern of fixing a 0.2% problem is that if you do fix the issue, how do you rapidly verify that the problem is actually corrected? Measuring a 0.2% failure rate requires a large number of products, and if the failure is a durability issue, it could take months or years to confirm the solution. A third concern is whether you actually know enough (or have learned enough) about the physics of the system to correct an issue that is not exhibited on 99.8% of your product. This whole illustration demonstrates the difficulty in achieving a quality rate of one issue per product, especially if you rely only on focus strategies.

Your goal is to make sure your product achieves high quality prior to shipment to your first customer. The goal of all problem solving is to detect and correct a problem before sending the product to your customers. If you attempt to complete your problem solving before you send the product into the field, not only will it be more difficult to solve the 0.2% problems, but you will have even more difficulty finding the 0.2% problem. Figure 9.4 shows the ability to find a problem based on an evaluation of 12–15 products (which may be unreasonable, but it is just for illustration purposes). The ability to detect a 1% problem (assuming the failure is an infant or random failure type) is less than 15%. The ability to detect a 0.5% failure rate (your most abundant-sized problem from Figure 9.3) is less than 1%.

Figures 9.3 and 9.4 demonstrate the issues associated with correction as you attempt to implement your quality plans.

To begin the journey of aggressive problem solving, you must follow a rigorous continuous improvement plan. I suggest a six-step plan of (1) establishing your improvement goals, (2) generating a list of problems to be worked along with the expected improvement contributions, (3) distributing the issues to the most appropriate owners (the people most likely to solve the issues quickly and with confidence; if at all possible, these people should be the people who designed the system), (4) driving rigorous problem solving using an established

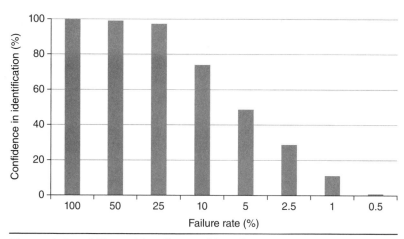

Figure 9.4 Ability to identify a problem (based on a small validation sample size of 12–15 products).

problem-solving process, (5) demanding verification to generate confidence in the solution, and finally (6) tracking the cumulative solutions to the goal.

There are several key attributes of this six-part procedure. First, your improvement goal must be based on customer-driven product quality improvement expectations. Although everyone has a list of the most pressing problems (including the plant managers and key executives), if customer information is available, use it to determine which problems to work first. Second, the problems worked on must not be just special cause problems or the boss's hit list. The problems and issues to be worked must be selected based on a Pareto of the most significant problems as identified by your customers. Third, you must use the existing people in your engineering, manufacturing, supplier, and sales groups. Fourth, standardized problem solving must be rigidly followed.

The standard problem-solving system must provide clear ownership of the problems and completion expectations. The problem-solving system must also provide a pull signal for escalating skills (there will be problems that require specialized skills that only a few employees possess). Lastly, the problem-solving system must emphasize process modification over product modification. Remember that most of your products are good and that something in the process allows some products to be good and some to be bad. To ensure compliance to your plan, you must provide education and training so that your employees have the required competencies.

Let's go back and review the details of the six problem-solving parts (pages 110–111). In part 1, your goals must be well defined and tied to your top leaders' expectations. Your leaders must recognize and get excited about achieving these goals. It doesn't make sense to drive a metric that nobody recognizes. Find out what excites your CEO and drive that. If your CEO does not get excited about any particular quality metric, you may have to educate him or her on the most appropriate customer metric.

In part 2, generate a list of problems to be worked to achieve your goal. I will start this discussion with a test. Let's say that I was recently on a company trip, and when I returned home my wife gave me a list of things that needed to be repaired or replaced. The list included the following items:

- Fallen tree branches from the last storm
- Garage needs to be swept out
- Tile in sunroom cracked
- TV remote control inoperative
- Bathroom door lock broken
- Grass growing in driveway cracks
- Lawn sprinkler head sprays erratically
- Hot water heater does not get hot enough
- Drywall nails pushing through the bedroom ceiling
- Front yard needs mowing

Which project should I do first and why?

This list was a quandary as I scheduled my Saturday activities. For my wife to be completely satisfied, all of the projects had to be completed, but I clearly did not have enough time for all of them. When looking at the problems, the first thing that must be asked is, who is prioritizing the work? In our example, if my wife were picking the projects, she would probably pick the hot water heater first because she doesn't like cold baths. On the other hand, I might pick the TV remote because, like most men, I don't want to get up to change the channel. If I hired someone to do the repairs, this individual might pick the easiest project first because his or her goal is to do as many jobs as possible in a short amount of time. The second question might be, what is the required outcome of the work? If I were trying to sell my house, mowing the lawn or picking up tree limbs might be the first project on the list, because nobody is going to stop and look at a house that is not maintained. A third question is, what skills are required to complete the list? Although I can take care of most items on the list, repairing cracked tile is something I might leave to professionals.

The purpose of this test is to illustrate the importance of ranking the issues that your company is working on. If engineers are picking the problems to be worked on, they may select easy issues with the goal of solving as many problems as possible in a short period of time. If your goal is to win in some external survey, picking the issues that the surveys highlight may be more beneficial, even if the problems are more difficult. Work on the issues that really matter to the customer, not the convenient ones.

In part 3, distribute the problems to the most appropriate owners. If at all possible, the problem owners should be those people who created the system or created parts within the system. Pick these people so that lessons are learned (more appropriately, physics is learned) and so these failures never occur in future designs. At the same time, be cautious: The engineers

who originally designed the system may have some precon-
ceived ideas about the true root cause. Make sure the engineers
are trained in problem solving and assign an advance problem
solver to the project at the first sign of a breakdown in problem-
solving logic.

In part 4, follow a problem-solving process that is commonly understood and applicable. Often, companies follow
many different problem-solving methods. Some of these have
limited logic. Watch out for the following attributes of poor
problem-solving processes: (1) problem solvers guessing at
solutions, (2) multiple changes being tried, (3) large meetings
and conference calls to talk and brainstorm, (4) just tracking
problems, hoping they will go away, (5) changing supplier
specifications without supporting logic, and (6) developing
theories and making changes to test the hypothesis one at a
time. These strategies will solve only the easiest of problems.
I prefer a problem-solving system that is driven by statistical confidence in each step. I call this statistical engineering.
No confidence can be achieved in your solution if there is
not first confidence in your root cause. The appendix contains
the complete statistical engineering analysis of an issue in a
vehicle assembly plant.

In part 5, verify that the solution actually fixes the issue.
Unfortunately, you cannot just go to the plant floor and see if
failures are occurring, since most of your problems are in the
field. Also, you do not want to wait for information from the
field; this could take months, and if the solution did not fix
the problem, you will have that many more dissatisfied customers. With the right problem-solving methodology, you can
establish a means to be able to turn the problem on and off and
verify that a problem is actually fixed. If your problem solvers
cannot demonstrate the ability to turn the problem on and off
but still have confidence in the solution, then look to the field
where the largest concentrations of failures occurred previously
and watch for the failure to go down there.

In part 6, track the solutions and improvements to your goal. Just as in any war strategy, you must track daily successes and failures so that corrective adjustments can be made to your quality plan. In this quality journey, quality knowledge is gained from wins and losses. I prefer a multilevel problem-solving process that combines containment, control, and correction. I recommend going back to the six-step problem-solving process in Chapter 8. These six steps will sort out the easily fixed control issues from the more difficult issues requiring engineering support to modify processes or designs. Just as the first three steps are for controlling the process, controlling the tools, and controlling the parts, steps four through six are for correcting different aspects of design. The three steps for correction are (1) correct the process, (2) correct the design, and (3) correct the fundamentals (the hardy perennials). These last three steps will provide the ability, with diligence and skills, to solve all of your most difficult problems. If you are just starting on your problem-solving journey, I suggest getting some professional support from experts.

The six-step problem-solving process shown in Figure 9.5 provides a well-thought-out and logical process for solving the easiest to the most complex problems. Each step in the process is identified by the type of action as well as the owner of that action. The first three steps concentrate on containment and control and are owned in manufacturing. The last three steps concentrate on correction (problem solving) and are owned by engineering.

Within the last three steps, step four is about changing the manufacturing and assembly process to eliminate the issue. Remember, most of your product does not have a problem. There is a reason some of your product is good and some is bad; usually the reason is contained in the process. Step five is about changing the product to eliminate the issue. Sometimes there is insufficient robustness in the process to correct the whole issue, and product changes will have to be made. Finally, step six is

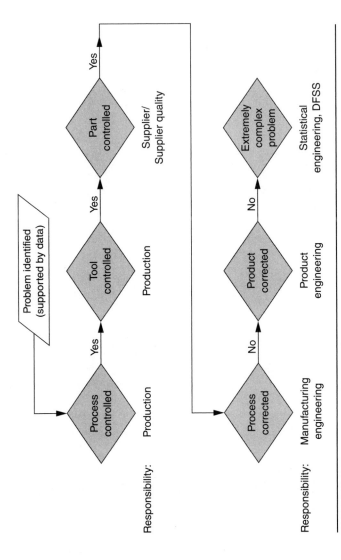

Figure 9.5 Six-step problem-solving process.

about changing the fundamental knowledge of failure for your extremely difficult problems and requires special skills to solve. Step six requires a more complete understanding of the physics of the failure and must be driven by a problem-solving master in partnership with the system design owners.

The six-step process follows an escalating progression of advancing tools to match the most difficult problems with the most advanced tools. Each step provides the quickest and cheapest solution with the highest solution confidence. Typically the contain/control steps (steps one through three) are essentially free. Corrective actions can be done rapidly and produce improvement with high levels of confidence.

Step four, also relatively free, involves changing the process to increase the percentage of defect-free products. The only costs would be for changing the assembly sequence, adding assembly tools and aids, or changing process parameters. Since only the process is being modified in this step, a high degree of confidence (95% confidence) is maintained. Step four takes slightly longer to fix than the first three steps since time must be spent finding good and bad products and following a problem-solving logic.

Step five involves changing the product design. This takes considerable time, requires significant investments, and generates lower confidence of correcting the problem the first time. Unfortunately, the redesign is often done by the same individual who originally designed and released the part. Rarely has that engineer gotten profound knowledge since the original design was released. Also remember that most of your problems are extremely infrequent in nature, maybe on the order of 1%–2%. The chances of creating an unknown problem with a frequency of 1% or 2% may be as high as or higher than your confidence in solving a 1%–2% problem.

Step six takes the longest time to correct and may cost the most money. Its resolution confidence can be high if the right tools are used to generate a correction. Resolution of step six issues almost always involves revisiting the physics of the system and determining a robust solution using advanced statistical engineering problem solving or DFSS.

Due to the low cost and high confidence, problem solving should be concentrated in steps one through four. I recommend that at least 70% of all problems be solved here. Sending problems to steps five and six should only be done if steps one through four cannot reduce the failure frequency to the desired level.

As I stated earlier, if a problem is found in the assembly plant, start with step one. If the problem is found in the field, you can still start the problem-solving process at step one, but it might be more effective to start at a higher step. There are numerous clues to look for when attempting to assign a problem within the six-step process.

Your sales and service personnel (sales and service are not on the six-step chart but are associated with step zero, identifying problems) may be assigned the task of helping select which problems should be worked as well as screening for legitimate problems. Sales and service should also be assigned problems associated with variation within the dealership or service centers. Typical issues to look for are the following:

- Dealership-to-dealership warranty variation
- High warranty prior to the product being sold to the customer
- Warranty associated with your service centers not following repair guidelines
- Transportation damage
- Ineffective service (high levels of customer concern that cannot be duplicated)
- Excessive goodwill—for example, a customer drops his cell phone in the lake and gets it replaced under warranty

Your manufacturing or assembly plants should be assigned the issue (steps one through three) if any of the following exist:

- Obvious process control problems

- Time-to-time variation (special cause issue in the most recent builds, versus previous builds)

- Early time to detect (the problem is detected within a couple months of usage)

- Plant-to-plant warranty variation

- Problem corrected by rebuilding or reassembling the component (no parts were replaced)

Your supplier should be assigned the issue (step three) if any of the following exist:

- Time-to-time variation

- Part-to-part variation (the same part is supplied by several suppliers, and one is good and one is bad)

- Warranty repair requires only replacing a part

Engineering should be assigned the issue (steps four through six) if any of the following exist:

- The problem cannot be fixed by steps one through three

- The problem is a wear-out or durability issue

- There is significant product-to-product variation (one cell phone model versus another cell phone model)

- Warranty differences due to geographic area

- Warranty differences due to variation in customer usage

- Problems caused by engineering product changes

The three key drivers of problem solving within any organization are engineering, manufacturing, and suppliers. Each organization provides key resources for the improvement of your product. Manufacturing and suppliers are responsible for solving problems that occur from variation within their build and assembly processes. They are responsible for ensuring that every product is built according to the prescribed process and that parts function as designed and are within specified tolerances.

Many companies follow a problem-solving process similar to the six-step process, but unfortunately many of these problem-solving processes do not contain a well-defined step four (statistical engineering) or step six (DFSS). Some companies have learned statistical engineering but use it only for problem definition and clue generation. My own belief is that the majority of problem solving should occur at the assembly or manufacturing location using steps one through four. Rarely should problem solving occur within product design (steps five and six).

The engineering center has the ability and the responsibility to solve problems, but it is more effective to solve problems by reducing the variation within the process. Reducing variation requires that problem solving occur where the product is being built. For most companies the majority of the problem solving occurs in the engineering center. One company I worked with was doing 70%–80% of its continuous improvement from the engineering center (step six). Although this much activity at the engineering center gave the appearance that much work was being done and generated great expectations for improvement, it did not produce the desired results. From my early estimates of success rates and cost, you can see in Table 9.1 that by driving improvements into steps five and six (product modification or redesign), you add considerable time, expense, and uncertainty to your improvement plan.

Step five should be used sparingly in production. Anytime it is used, it should be preceded by step four. In other words, you should use statistical engineering (step four) to define the cause of the problems and generate a solution. Step five (redesign) should be used to actually design the change, establish

Table 9.1 Six-step improvement statistics.

Step	Action	Improvement	Confidence in improvement	Cost	Time
1	Process control	Small	High	Low	Fast
2	Tool control	Small	High	Low	Fast
3	Part control	Small	High	Low	Fast
4	Process correction	Medium	High	Low	Moderate
5	Product correction	Large	Medium*	Medium	Slow*
6	Fundamentals correction	Significant	Low*	High	Very slow

*Can be improved with proper leadership, strategy, and tools.

specifications, and release the change. Statistical engineering should again be used to demonstrate that the problem has been killed. Step five should rarely be used by itself; when it is used independently, engineers often guess at solutions.

To verify that your organization is solving problems in the most effective way, look for signs of ineffective problem solving:

1. Are multiple changes required to solve a problem? Killing a problem requires one change, sometimes two; rarely does it take three or more changes to kill a problem. If multiple changes are being implemented, you may actually be increasing the chance of deteriorating quality by introducing buds of problems (more on buds in the next chapter).

2. Do you hear engineers say, "I think," "I hope," "My engineering judgment is . . . ," or "Let's try this change"? If so, your engineers are guessing at solutions. Although hope is fantastic for many things, it makes for a very poor problem-solving methodology.

3. Are your engineers able to turn the problem on and off?
   If the root cause is truly determined, you will be able to
   turn the problem off with the change and turn the problem back on when you change back. If the problem
   cannot be turned off and on like a light switch, then
   confidence in problem closure is minimal.

Often, even when a manufacturing and/or assembly process is
precisely followed, failures occur. If the exact processes are
being followed but failures still occur, step four (statistical
engineering problem solving) is an effective process for determining which factors or characteristics contribute to the failure.
It can determine the one part or process that is bad and confirm
the parts or processes that are good. Dorian Shainin once told
me that if I could make one good product, he could show me
how to make all of them good. I am not sure that I am that good
of a problem solver, but I do know that there are quantifiable
reasons that good and bad products are made from the same
parts and processes. I have found that the quickest way to find
them is through statistical engineering. Statistical engineering
is modeled after a process developed by Shainin LLC called
the "Red X" process.

A key illustration from Dorian Shainin was the dictionary
game. In this game, you picked one word from the dictionary
(there are about 120,000 words in my dictionary), and with no
more than 17 questions he could pick the word that you had
selected. He would first ask, "Does the letter begin with 'L' or
above?" Although this question never identified the word, it
eliminated about 60,000 words. If the answer was "above L,"
he would then ask, "Is the first letter L through Q?" With this
question an additional 30,000 words were eliminated. After no
more than 17 guesses, 119,999 words were eliminated, and the
one remaining word was the one you had picked. As you've
likely detected, a key part of statistical engineering is eliminating the causes that are not part of the problem.

The first time you play the dictionary game, someone will likely ask whether the word is a verb or a noun. Although all words in the dictionary are identified as a part of speech, it is not organized that way. The "physics" of the dictionary is that it is organized alphabetically. Now you need to ask what the physics of your products are. One clear property is that parts are received and then assembled. Therefore, one question that can be asked is, does the problem follow the parts or the assembly process? The physics of your system (cause of variability) may be part to part, shift to shift, operator to operator, assembly line to assembly line, plant to plant, time to time, or some other unique physical attributes of your products. Try to understand the physics of the variables that can produce performance variation before you attempt to solve problems.

The statistical engineering process relies on asking questions that are supported by the physics of the system. The physics of a dictionary is in how it is organized: alphabetically. Dorian Shainin always told me to talk to the parts—they are trying to communicate with you. But just like learning French or German, it takes time and practice to be proficient in any language. I'm sure that with some of the problems I have worked on, the parts were yelling at me, but I was too blockheaded to hear them.

Although Red X as created by Dorian Shainin has been around for just over 50 years, the logic has been around for centuries. There are several great examples of using statistical engineering principles in the field of medicine. The first was in the determination of a cure for smallpox. In the late nineteenth century, Edward Jenner set out to find a cure for smallpox. The first thing he needed to understand was who gets smallpox and who does not. He needed to find a contrast (BOBs and WOWs). After repeatedly hearing "Everyone gets it," he finally found the contrast he was looking for: Milkmaids did not get smallpox. Jenner did not understand immunity, white blood cells, viruses, or vaccines. But he understood that he needed to find a solution, that the problem was complex, and that he would never be able to understand everything. He also understood that he needed to find a contrast. And this contrast led to a vaccine for smallpox.

What can we learn from Edward Jenner?

- Stay focused on defining the problem

- Look for contrasts

- Question existing facts

- Do not try to understand everything; you only need to find out what drives the contrast

- Find the answer from the location of the problem, not from your desk

- Understand that there will always be "noise"

The second medical example was in the discovery of the cause of cholera. Just like Jenner, James Snow wanted to find the cause of a disease that had afflicted the population for eternity. Many others had attempted to find the cause in the past, and many different theories were taught. Let's look at the principles learned from Jenner that Snow used:

- Stay focused on defining the problem—600 people died within a quarter mile radius in a few days in 1854.

- Look for contrasts—most deaths occurred around one water pump on Broad Street, with the exception of the people who collected their water from the work house or brewery. Both the work house and brewery had their own water supply (see Figure 9.6).

- Question existing facts—cholera could not be airborne, as taught by medical experts, since Snow treated patients without ever catching it.

- Do not try to understand everything; you only need to find out what drives the contrast—patients' pain was in

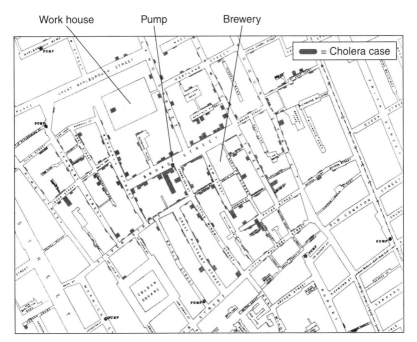

Figure 9.6   London cholera outbreak of 1854.

the gut, so the affliction must be ingested, not inhaled; given the speed and severity of the outbreak, the culprit must live in something commonly used by most residents.

- Find the answer from the location of the problem, not from your desk—during the outbreak, Snow gathered clues from the Soho slums, not from his office.

- Understand that there will be "noise"—two women living five miles away died, but they drank water from the Broad Street pump.

Statistical engineering is a way of thinking. It is based on statistics, engineering sciences, logic, creativity, and persistence. In our partitioning of strategies between focus and APAT, statistical engineering is a key focus strategy. It relies on the assumption that for every problem there is a Pareto of causes. Statistically it can be shown that the largest contributors can be quickly determined with some basic statistical tools and logical thought. Statistical engineering is not just another set of DOE techniques; it typically uses very simple statistical tools created by Dorian Shainin or other statisticians and engineers. It looks for contrasts to solve problems. Emphasis is on the ability to explain why a failure is occurring. To truly eliminate a problem you must understand the physics of the failure. Demonstration of the knowledge of the physics of failure requires the ability to turn the problem on and off with high statistical confidence.

The following are the guiding principles of statistical engineering:

- There is a Pareto of causes for every variation effect; tighter control of anything other than the most important factors gives little return.

- You need to talk to the parts—leverage the difference between really good and bad parts or processes.

- Progressive search—start with an open mind and throw out those things that do not fit the clues (e.g., the 119,999 words in the dictionary that were not the one picked). As Sherlock Holmes said to Dr. Watson, "Eliminate all other factors, and the one which remains must be the truth. How often have I said to you that when you have eliminated the impossible, whatever remains, however improbable, must be the truth?"

Statistical engineering strategy basics are as follows:

- In order to learn about any problem, we must be able to measure it. Measuring things is a fundamental practice of translating customer expectations into engineering requirements.

- If you make good products and bad products, there is a reason.

- More important, if you make good products and bad products, then you *can* make all good products.

- There are techniques to help find the *true* root cause of a problem.

Statistical engineering is not just about finding solutions to problems; it is about gaining technical knowledge on how systems really work. Knowledge is typically communicated from experts. Often experts give us too much information, and the information is driven by their opinions and emotions. Facts and fiction are confused. True knowledge is gained through experience, asking questions, and observing the results. The secret to successfully gaining knowledge is strategically asking questions with factual responses. As Albert Einstein stated, "We can't solve problems by using the same kind of thinking we used when we created them."

The great news about problem solving is that there are typically only two types of problems:

- Physics—Something does not work

  — Doesn't function

  — Doesn't perform the way it was intended

- Geometry—Something does not fit

  — Gaps, flushness, contour

  — Interference

  — Position

There are six steps within the statistical engineering process:

1. Listen to the customer (your customer is the final judge of the goodness of your product)

2. Observe the failure

3. Measure the contrast

4. Determine the major contributor

5. Confirm the contributor (make the appropriate changes)

6. Implement control or change

I have highlighted the importance of "measuring it" because within focus strategies, it is important to have statistical confidence in the solutions to your problems. Your measurement system must be repeatable and discriminate between your BOBs and WOWs. Typically, measurement confidence is provided by means of an isoplot (see Figure 9.7).

An *isoplot* is a statistical method of demonstrating confidence in your measurement system. It validates that your measurement variation is significantly less than your product variation. Therefore, as you modify your product or process, you can have confidence that any changes seen will be produced by the product and not by the measurement system.

An isoplot is generated by measuring your product multiple times. Typically 30 products, which make up your range

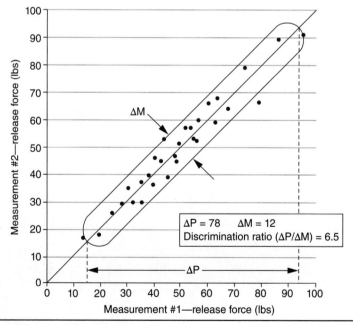

Figure 9.7   Isoplot example.

of variation, are measured twice. Each pair of measurements is plotted on the graph, with the first measurement plotted along the horizontal axis and the second measurement plotted along the vertical axis. After all pairs are plotted, a box is drawn around 29 of the 30 points (for 95% confidence). The width of the box (perpendicular to the slope) is the measurement fluctuation. The distance on the horizontal axis from the extreme points is the product variation. To have 95% confidence in your measurement system, the ratio of product variation to measurement variation must be at least 6.

Typical problem solving (non–statistical engineering) begins with brainstorming sessions. The purpose of these sessions is to generate large numbers of possible causes (the more the better). The possible causes are tried one at a time until the problem is solved. This problem-solving process is judged on the basis of how many possible causes are identified and the rate at which solutions are evaluated. This problem-solving process can be divergent in that much of the activity can lead you away from the true solution. This type of problem solving is costly, very time consuming, and often does not lead to a solution. I call this X to Y problem solving. The X represents possible solutions, and the Y represents the resulting change to the customer attribute. Although this approach must be used when you are creating a new product, it should be avoided when solving an existing problem.

$$Y = X_1 + X_2 + X_3 + X_4 + X_5 + X_6 + \ldots + X_n$$

Y = the engineering specification that most closely reflects the customer desire

X = the factors that may (or may not) drive the improvement of Y

Another drawback is that, as mentioned earlier in the isoplot discussion, you need to have confidence that changes you evaluate are true changes and not fluctuations in your measurement system. Typically only the two or three most significant factors will pass an isoplot. Factors smaller than the top three have less magnitude than that generated within your measurement system. Essentially your measurement system for the lesser factors is a random number generator. Therefore, the thought of looking at each factor one at a time cannot really be accomplished.

A preferred process goes from Y to X. Strategies must be formulated that eliminate *groups* of factors that may not have any impact on Y. If enough factors are eliminated (just as words were eliminated in the dictionary example), then whatever factors remain must contribute to the Y. To do so, you must look for differences in various causes (Xs) at the extremes of the effect (Y) to progressively narrow in on the one cause (X) that drives the variation. The final cause (X_1) must make sense relative to the physics of the problem. Remember that all problems have one major factor, *sometimes* there is a second contributor (X_2), but rarely are there three or more contributors.

A great example of statistical engineering problem solving was at a vehicle assembly plant that had problems within its painting operation: Some painted parts had small defects called fish eyes. When alerted to the situation, I immediately got on a plane and traveled to the plant. When I got there I saw that a typical problem-solving session had begun. About 30 people were crammed into a room designed for 20, and they were identifying all of the reasons that fish eyes could occur. Their brainstorming list of possible causes included several hundred issues. The statistical engineering master who accompanied me immediately dismissed 27 people, keeping only the operator, the foreman, and a material expert. Figure 9.8 is a partial list of the items that were generated.

Understanding the physics of painting, the first question the master asked was, "Are the fish eyes on all paint colors?" The answer was yes, eliminating paint contamination because each paint color was mixed and contained separately (about

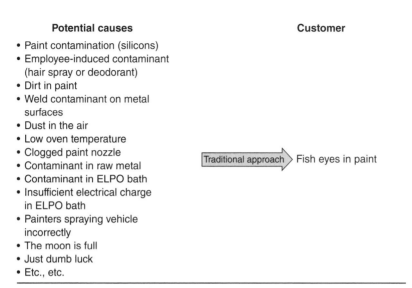

Figure 9.8 X to Y thinking example.

20 causes). The second question was, "Are the fish eyes in all of the panels?" The answer was no. Since the whole vehicle is painted in one operation, the paint booth was eliminated as the cause of the problem (about 40 causes from the brainstorming list). Next he asked, "Are the fish eyes on horizontal surfaces?" Again, no. This eliminated the 20 questions on the paint booth cleaning that had occurred several weeks before, causing dust to fall on the freshly painted car. Next he asked, "Are there any specific panels that show more fish eyes?" They stated that the rear quarter panel had the largest number of fish eyes. Records were obtained that showed the panel had recently been sourced from a new supplier.

The problem with the fish eyes lived in the quarter panel from the new supplier, not in the assembly plant. The plant immediately switched back to the previous supplier, and the fish eyes went away. With the knowledge that the fish eyes lived in the quarter panel, the statistical engineering master immediately got on a plane to visit the panel supplier and within a week was able to find the filter that was plugged in the metal processing operation. It is interesting to note that no one in the brainstorming session had suggested that a filter at the metal supplier might be plugged.

Statistical engineering follows a Y to X methodology. Questions are asked not to find the solution but to eliminate the hundreds of causes that are not the solution (see Figure 9.9).

Statistical engineering is similar to the process followed by Sherlock Holmes. His goal was to eliminate all of the people who could not have possibly committed the crime. When enough suspects were eliminated, the criminal could be easily determined through association with the clues. The perpetrator of the crime always has unique characteristics associated with the crime, and there is usually only one suspect that fits the character of all the clues.

The statistical engineering strategies are great for rapidly improving the quality of your products, but there are some drawbacks. One drawback is when your BOB is not good enough. Improving your product to the best-of-the-best level, although a significant accomplishment, may not be enough to satisfy your customers. To improve beyond this level may require some

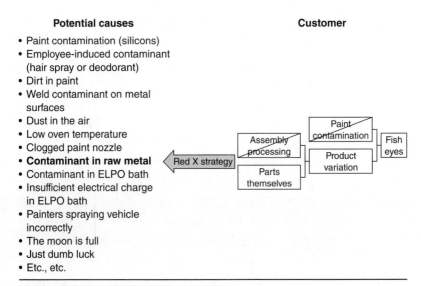

Figure 9.9 Y to X thinking example.

creation tools, described in the next chapter. A second drawback is that the statistical engineering strategies look at parts or processes that currently exhibit variability. If a part or process does not vary, by definition of the Red X it cannot be the prime contributor. If additional variables are thought to contribute, the statistical engineering strategies can still be used, but only by forcing artificial variation into these possible contributors.

In the appendix is an example of a statistical engineering project that was given to me by a friend. He used this example to show the benefits of statistical engineering over typical trial-and-error approaches. Determine whether your problem solving follows this logic or whether it is more trial and error.

As problems are identified, root causes found, and solutions created, the problems can be placed into several categories (see Figure 9.10). The first category is for those problems where the root cause is known and solutions are being implemented. For these projects, you should implement the solution quickly, track the quality improvement, and celebrate the win. The second category includes problems where the root cause is known but solutions are *not* being implemented.

The reasons for no action are numerous, but from my experience, the most prevalent is piece-cost or investment. The typical direction given to the engineer is to find a different solution

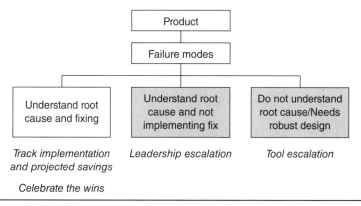

Figure 9.10   Failure mode escalation.

(e.g., a less costly solution): "I don't like solution A; find solution B." Sometimes different solutions are possible, but often solution A is the only solution ($X_2 + X_3$ rarely equals the value of X_1). If no other solutions can be found, the problems in this bucket need to be escalated to senior leadership for roadblock removal. We call this *leadership escalation*. The reason for the impasse is due to the comparison of the cost of implementing an engineering solution versus the cost of quality. We must remember that the cost of quality is typically much greater than the warranty cost alone. Most quality books identify the cumulative internal costs of quality (hard to measure) as being equal to the cumulative external costs that are easily measured. Unfortunately, this explanation of external and internal quality costs is not usually taught in business school; therefore, senior leadership must be engaged to break these roadblocks. Everyone knows the importance of high-quality products. In the APAT example of employee safety discussed in Chapter 4, there was very little discussion of whether you should spend money to prevent an accident; it was a given. This same mentality must prevail if you plan on becoming the quality leader to your customers.

The last bucket is for problems where no solution is found. For these problems, escalation to more advanced problem solving is required. We call this *tool escalation*. These three buckets should make up the total problems that must be solved to meet your quality goal. As an organization matures in a culture of quality and the skill levels of the engineers increase, the leadership escalation bucket may go away.

While I am fond of the statistical engineering tool, I also have to provide a warning. Although it is a great tool, it is not appropriate for all problem-solving needs, and there are some issues that require more sophisticated tools.

Although I have talked primarily about statistical engineering as a focus strategy within this chapter on correction, there are numerous APAT problem-correction strategies that can be implemented. Many attributes of statistical engineering can be applied by all the people, all the time. In almost every problem-solving situation I have been involved in, the operator was deeply involved and was very aware of differences in the parts he or she saw, as well as how the process was done differently between shifts. The front line for all problem solving is at the operator station. Teach the basics of statistical problem solving to the operators. Teach them to look for clues such as time, process step, temperature, location, and so forth. All clues will come in handy when a trained observer reviews them. All parts pass through the operators; therefore, the process is best conducted here.

In evaluating the production process of a competitor, I was reviewing some control charts. On the control chart, the quality level was stationary, around four or five failures per day, as measured in the final plant audit. Someone had written "reinstruct the operator" on the chart. Although reinstructing the operator is never wrong, it is a very incomplete quality strategy. Since the quality level was stable (neither improving nor deteriorating), this suggests to me that the operator was probably doing the job according to the prescribed instructions. A better strategy would be to instruct the operator on some basic statistical engineering principles. Teach the operator to look for failure patterns: time of failure, part variability, difficulty of assembly, or noticeable changes in the assembly tools or equipment. The operator can usually describe in detail when air pressures are low or tools are wearing. Help the operator understand the physics of failure. You will be pleasantly surprised by the value of all operators being involved in solving problems. An additional benefit is job satisfaction. Everyone wants to be part of the process of improvement.

Kepner-Tregoe problem solving and basic quality skills such as the 5 Whys should be taught to all operators. While one operator solving a very small problem may be insignificant, hundreds of operators solving small problems becomes very significant.

When a new product is just starting production, the majority of your problems will be in steps four through six (probably over 50%). As your quality improves, more and more of the improvement will come through control and less through correction. Control (or more appropriately, the lack of control) will take on an ever-increasing role in your quality journey. Figure 9.11 depicts your product quality as a flowing stream. Initially the boulders in the stream (control problems) are hidden by the high water levels (overall poor quality). These control problems may produce a ripple, but the major flow is driven by your inherent product quality. As your product quality associated with design improves (the water level recedes), the inherent quality problems associated with poor control become more visible.

As your quality improves you may sense that your manufacturing operations are getting more and more out of control.

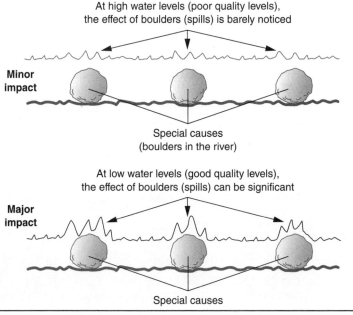

Figure 9.11 Effect of special cause problems (quality spills) on overall quality.

This is not the case. It is just that issues that may have been hidden in the past are now visible due to your improvements. Elimination of these control problems must follow the six-step problem-solving process.

The interpretation of this phenomenon is that your quality plan must follow a rigorous process that matches the most appropriate tools and resources with the associated problems. You must maintain a balance of containment, control, and correction.

Use the entire problem-solving process to drive quality to the highest level possible.

> *Correct (or correction) is about the permanent elimination of existing problems. Correction has the ability to produce great product quality improvement. Correction is problem solving using a wide variety of tools, but it is most effective by determining the differences in parts or process that produce different levels of customer attributes. Problem solving should be driven at every level, from the plant floor to the experts in engineering.*

ADDITIONAL READING

Bhote, K. R., and A. Bhote. 2000. *World Class Quality: Using Design of Experiments to Make It Happen.* New York: American Management Association.

Koch, R. 2008. *The 80/20 Principle: The Secret to Success by Achieving More with Less.* New York: Doubleday.

10

Create

Create

This chapter discusses and reviews the create (or creation) category of quality formation. A brief definition of creation is provided as well as some of the author's experiences. Included in the chapter are both focus and APAT strategies you can implement to start your own creation program.

*C*reate, or *creation*, is conceiving or modifying designs and processes that generate enthusiastic customers. It is the generation of products that are robust. Robust designs deliver more than expected. Robust designs satisfy the wide range of customer expectations and are insensitive to manufacturing and assembly variation. Robust designs *do not fail* in the customers' usage period. Creation has the ability to fundamentally change your product. As John Foster Dulles stated, "The measure of success is not whether you have a tough problem to deal with, but whether it's the same problem you had last year."

Creation provides the greatest level of quality at the lowest cost and investment. Creation consumes about 5% of expenses in the development process but generates about 70% of the influence (see Figure 10.1).

Most companies either do not understand this concept or fail to understand how to take advantage of it. In most cases, manpower is assigned to new product development after the time of greatest influence has passed. Creation should cause us to rethink the assigning of manpower (see Figure 10.2).

Creation often takes the greatest amount of time to implement because a new design must be created. For this reason, if

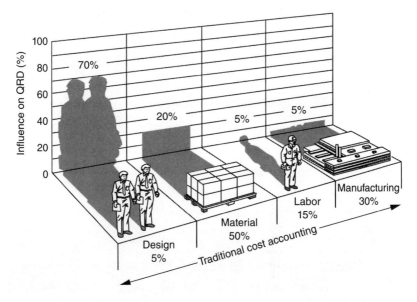

Product design influences the quality of a product more than any other factor

Figure 10.1 Impact on quality, reliability, and durability (QRD).

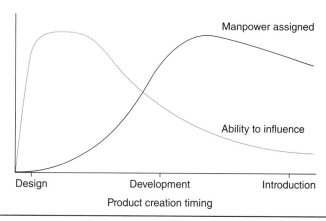

Figure 10.2 Engineering resources.

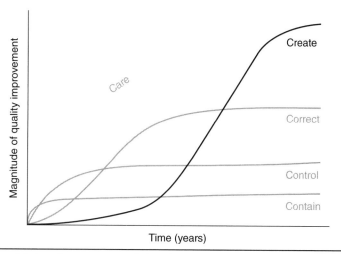

Figure 10.3 Create—one of the Five Cs.

creation is delayed, opportunities can and will be missed. Creation is not just about generating new and robust products; it is also about reusing robust products and keeping existing robust products robust. Figure 10.3 shows the significant improvement from creation over correction, as well as the additional time required to begin to achieve it. Creation can double or even triple your improvement rate, but at the cost of design and development time to implement.

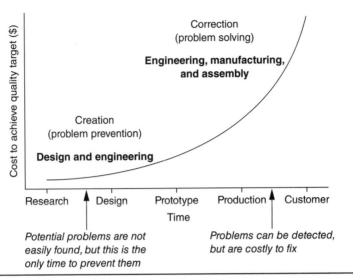

Figure 10.4 Comparison—correction versus creation.

A comparison of the costs to achieve your quality objective versus time is shown in Figure 10.4. In correction, problems are easy to see but costly to fix. In creation, problems are hard to see, but this may be the only time to prevent them. Creation is done in the research and design stages; correction is done in the prototype and production stages. The cost to prevent problems is relatively low, whereas the cost to fix problems is very high, especially if the problem is not detected prior to production.

Creation is the most underutilized, misunderstood, and poorly executed of all the initiatives. In the first four initiatives (care, contain, control, and correct), improvement is easily seen and measured, and thus most companies reward actions in the first four Cs. Even with significant activity in care, contain, control, and correct, you will still be sending problems on to your customers (never forget that your customers strongly object to being your test or validation engineer). If you truly plan on being a world-class quality producer, you must have significant activity in create.

Improvement within creation is more abstract, less visual, and more difficult to quantify. The evidence of improvement from the first four initiatives is often demonstrated by actual hardware. You build it and break it (or your customers break it), fix it, and then learn from it. In creation, the evidence is often demonstrated in the math or in the virtual realm. Creation robustness is often demonstrated in virtual predictions and comparisons of averages, standard deviations, and signal-to-noise ratios. Even though you may be uncomfortable with the lack of hardware, this should not necessarily reduce your confidence in the quality of the design. The ability to influence a design is not when a product's hardware has been produced; it is when the concepts are being discussed. Due to a lack of metrics and understanding, manpower is typically assigned much later in the design process.

The challenge of assigning manpower requires great faith during the first product development cycle. This faith should not be based on false hopes or partial plans. Extensive analysis of all parts and systems must be initiated and a detailed robustness plan created. Robustness leaders and tool experts must be assigned and provided goals. Systems must be put in place to review progress and make adjustments to the overall plan. Just like a snowball rolling downhill, success will drive success. With each successful plan execution, robustness masters will be trained, and the movement of manpower into the development cycle will become easier.

Creation is a key ingredient in the Juran trilogy. Robustness is the inherent quality of the initial design. In the Juran trilogy, it is the very first point on the glide path (see Figure 10.5). The activities that occur between the robustness point and the launch line are a combination of creation and correction in the pre-production phase (find the problems and fix them). The lower the robustness point, the higher the quality will be at launch and in production. If your robustness point is too high, significant problem solving will be required during the design and development period. Problem solving is always driven by finding and fixing failures. Finding failures is handicapped by

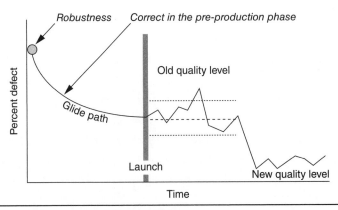

Figure 10.5   Juran quality model.

the fact that most problem solving is hardware driven and very little hardware exists during pre-production. For durability-type problems, you may run a small number of samples. These samples can provide confidence in your long-term quality by generating information that can be plotted on a Weibull chart. Unfortunately, sufficient information to generate a Weibull chart is not necessarily enough to modify your quality plan and identify all of the weak systems. If your pre-production quality is not sufficient, additional samples may have to be tested.

Multiple Environment Overstress Testing may draw system weaknesses out of your design. Unfortunately, for infant mortality and random failure portions of the failure bathtub curve your confidence is based on an attribute: "it failed" or "it did not fail." This requires large sample sizes in order to gain confidence. However, these large sample sizes may not be available, or they may be present only just prior to production. Any failure that is detected, due to the limited ability to detect a problem, signifies a catastrophe. For this reason, every effort must be made to drive the robustness point as low as possible. If you miss this opportunity, you are destined for much hard work, finding and fixing failures later on.

As in the discussion on correction, create must be simplified to be executable. It can be broken down into the following four steps: establish robust target, use robust, make robust, and

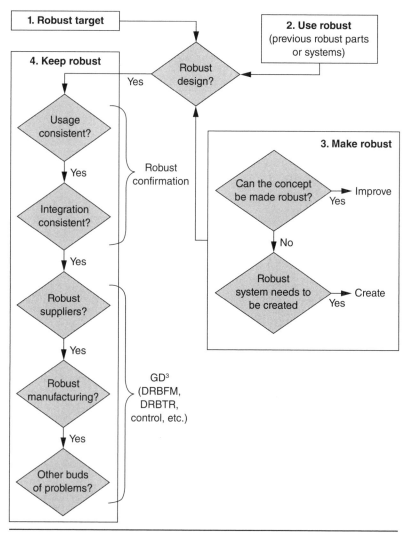

Figure 10.6 Problem prevention process.

keep robust, as shown in Figure 10.6. This chart might also be called the "seven diamonds of robustness" for the seven questions that must be asked.

As stated earlier, not only does creation have the ability to provide the most benefit, it is the only methodology that achieves improvement without your customers defining your problems in the field (although customer information is always required up front to establish critical wins as well as performance expectations).

These seven diamonds of robustness are applicable for components, subsystems, systems, or processes. As in correction, robust targets must first be established. These targets are established from customer expectations and competitor performance. Determining the target is often difficult for sublevels such as component or subsystem but is more easily determined for the total system. From the total system expectations, assumptions for individual components will have to be made such that the robustness of the total number of systems is equivalent to the total system.

Tools such as quality function deployment (QFD) and loss function analysis should be used to assist in the determination of customer robustness expectations. These expectations should be compared against your competitor's performance to establish their correctness. Since the target is always moving (improving), anticipate where your competitor will be and shoot ahead of it. Be very careful: Your customers are fickle and are apt to change as new products are introduced. Once the target is established, the next step is to determine whether any components or systems you are currently using meet your quality expectations. The available systems will fall into three categories: (1) always robust, (2) sometimes robust, and (3) never robust. Systems that are always robust are obviously the best to reuse. With the right tools and understanding, sometimes-robust systems may be reused. Don't overlook the components and systems your competitor uses; they may also be available.

If you have systems that are robust to your customer expectations, determine their performance bandwidth. By *bandwidth*, I mean the range of control (e.g., torque, temperature, and time) and noise factors (e.g., mass, voltage, current, and loading) that the system is robust within. Outside this bandwidth, the robustness is undetermined and may be poor. In Figure 10.7 four systems are used on 16 products. The always-

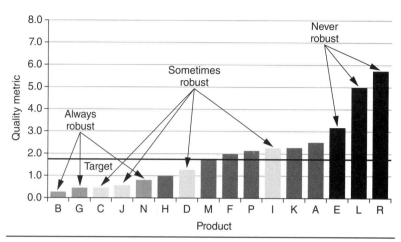

Figure 10.7 System or component performance.

robust system is used on only three products. Make sure you understand the characteristics of these three products. Any significant change outside the noise and control bandwidth could result in a less than desired performance. If you do go outside your noise or control boundaries, you must assess whether the system maintains its robustness.

If at all possible, keep within the preestablished bandwidth. A catalog of parts and systems should be created that identifies the part (or system) and the range of the noise factors and control that the systems are robust within. A catalog of processes should also be created that identifies manufacturing and assembly processes, along with the conditions that these processes are robust to.

Reusing robust systems is critical to any successful quality strategy. The systems that satisfy your customers' expectations require no engineering resources to redesign or investment to retool. Although you may feel that your company has few systems that are truly robust, you may be surprised. Remember, almost all of your conversations and meetings are engaged with systems that are not robust and need improvement. Think of the systems that you never talk about; they are probably your most robust. Look also at your competitor's systems and determine whether they are robust.

One method for assessing the robustness of a system is with a tool called robust assessment. It is one of the tools within DFSS. It uses an ideal function with the preestablished noise and control factors and statistically determines which competing system is more robust. Robust assessment may also be used as a simple DOE with the current and future noise and control parameters included to determine the robustness outside bandwidth limits.

If a robust system is not available, then it must be created from the ground up or through improving a nonrobust system. Be cautious: Systems that are robust in some applications *may not* be robust in other applications. A great example is car brakes. A braking system that meets all of your customer expectations in one vehicle may not meet them at all when used in a vehicle that weighs 50 kg more. Likewise, a CD player that plays retail music extremely well may have difficulties playing CDs made from a home computer. The robustness of a system under different control factors and environments is called performance bandwidth. Figure 10.8 show the performance bandwidth for one component on several different products.

In Figure 10.9, a system is robust in three applications but not in others. Make sure a complete understanding exists for the boundary conditions, environment factors, noise factors, or other circumstances that cause this system to not meet your targeted quality levels.

If a system can be found that is robust under some conditions, as shown in Figure 10.9, then tools may be applied that determine the factors that allow a system to be robust under some more strenuous or different conditions. Two tools that I have found most helpful are statistical engineering and DFSS. Statistical engineering looks for the factor that has the most significant contribution. This factor is called the "Red X." Movement or control of the Red X has the greatest ability to improve

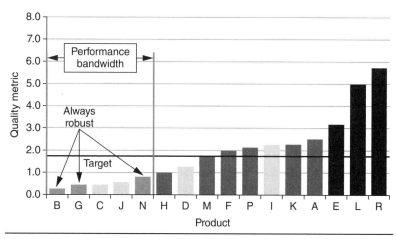

Figure 10.8 Performance bandwidth.

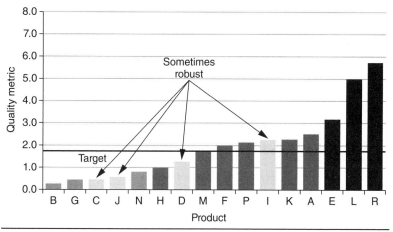

Figure 10.9 System that may be made robust.

the design. Likewise, the second most important factor is the "Pink X," and the third most important is the "Pale Pink X." Unfortunately, classical statistical engineering methodology looks only at factors that vary. If a factor does not vary, it cannot be the Red X, even though it could have great product influence. Fortunately, since BOBs and WOWs can be found, and factors that vary cause the variation, the statistical engineering methodology almost always works (and a Red X is found).

DFSS has the additional advantage of looking for the influence of factors that do not vary. DFSS can look at many factors and conditions (system noise and control factors) and optimize the design to be robust under these conditions. In this case of optimizing a current design, only a small portion of the DFSS tool kit is required (more to come on the total tool kit). By optimizing the design around the key design factor or combination of factors, you may be able to expand the performance bandwidth.

If no systems are available that meet your performance bandwidth requirements, a new system will need to be created. In our four-step robustness diagram that was shown in Figure 10.6, creating a new system is called "make robust." DFSS is an ideal tool to make systems robust. DFSS can actually be looked at as a series of tools that, when combined, lead to robust systems. As shown in Figure 10.10, five steps make up DFSS and go by the acronym IDDOV: identify the opportunity, define the requirements, develop the concept, optimize the design, and verify and launch the design.

Since there are numerous great books on DFSS, I will give only a cursory overview. Let's look at each of the steps in a little more detail. In the first step you identify the opportunity or challenge. You define the scope and charter of a project and develop a team to establish an action plan. The team must include a dedicated leader, an experienced DFSS expert (typically a DFSS Black Belt or Master Black Belt), and sufficient team members to support the completion of the project. Each of these members must be fully committed to the project, and the leader must understand that the success or failure of the project will be directly affected by his or her ability to lead and support the team. In the second step you establish the customer needs and wants and translate these into engineering metrics. These needs and wants must be prioritized to reflect customer importance—that is, how important or critical they are to the ultimate customer—key buying factors, regulatory requirements, business imperatives, and competitor assessment. To help organize the information, a

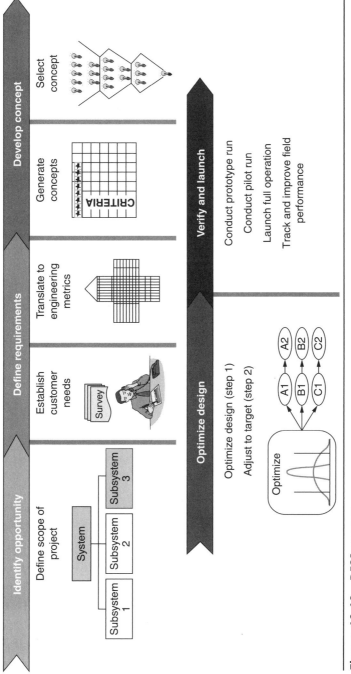

Figure 10.10 DFSS process.

"House of Quality" is typically built. The House of Quality assists in translating customer desires into engineering metrics. Targets will then need to be set on all engineering metrics so that the team has a clear understanding of success.

In the third step you generate multiple concepts to satisfy the customer requirements. This step takes great creativity; hopefully your team includes people from multiple disciplines who are very broad minded. Be careful of engineers who think they already know the optimum solution. The leader must challenge the team to look at competitor solutions as well as systems from totally different products (e.g., auto manufacturers can learn significant lessons from aircraft or appliance manufacturers). When a large list of possible solutions is identified, see if the solutions can be mixed and matched to make totally different solutions. At the completion of this step, the most probable concept to optimize should be selected. You may use Pugh analysis to generate, analyze, and quantify competing concepts.

In the fourth step you use DOE and other tools to evaluate your design proposal. All factors must be evaluated and have their sensitivity determined, and any interactions must also be identified. This information must be used to optimize your design and adjust your targets.

In the final step, you finalize operations and service processes, produce prototype and pilot systems, and launch and observe the performance. The verification step is about closing the loop and confirming that the opportunity that was originally identified and the requirements that were established were achieved.

You have now progressed in the four steps to robustness to either having selected a robust system or having created one. You must now make sure that the system remains robust, or as Figure 10.6 explains, "keep it robust." During the design and development process, changes often occur. Mass, environmental loading, interface connectivity, manufacturing processes, and even suppliers may change. The question that must be asked is, will your robust system remain robust after these changes? Tatsuhiko Yoshimura identifies these changes as the producers of buds of problems. Whenever change is introduced, a bud is created. In most cases these buds never bloom or produce an undesirable consequence. But in a small percentage of changes, the bud blooms into a significant stinkweed. These stinkweeds can create significant issues in your manufacturing operations or, even worse, with your customers.

The first type of change to be concerned with is that which changes the noise factors of your system—essentially, factors that place your product outside normal or historical operation. Noise factors can be broken into categories of customer usage, environmental influences, supplier and manufacturing variation, connecting system variation, and natural aging or wear. Although these variations may be significantly outside your control, you will need to be diligent about making sure you understand and comprehend your products' robustness to them. For these changes, a quick look using DFSS is recommended to verify the robustness of the system under these new conditions. In this case, an ideal tool within DFSS is robust confirmation. *Robust confirmation* provides a quick look at whether a system is maintaining its robustness. Robust confirmation uses the ideal function and looks at changes to either the noise or the control factors to determine whether the robustness ratio or the signal-to-noise ratio has changed. For noise factors such as supplier changes, manufacturing changes, or minor design changes, GD^3 is recommended. GD^3 is similar to review processes such as DFMEA and PFMEA, with the exception that you concentrate on changes at the interface between components or systems. GD^3 requires a complete review of the changes with a team of engineers, suppliers, and other experts with the desire to find and correct any fault that may produce an undesirable outcome.

The second type of change to be concerned with is that which changes the control factors of your system—essentially, factors you control that may be outside the normal and historical manufacturing and assembly process ranges. Control factors can typically be broken into the same categories as in an Ishikawa (fishbone) diagram: manpower control, machine control, and material control. Just like in noise control, any control factors that are outside the normal and historical operating range must be assumed to produce a bud of a problem and be verified by robust confirmation.

In the prior four Cs—care, contain, control, and correct— the APAT strategy was deemed to be an important aid in the maturity of the quality strategy. In create, APAT is essential, and GD^3 in particular is critical to the success of the strategy. Unfortunately, as good as DFSS can be in driving a robust design, there will still be noise and control factors outside the scope of the analysis. To get that last bit of robustness into your design, APAT must become part of your robust design process.

As stated earlier, defining quality problems before they occur is translated in Japanese as *Mizenboushi*. Mizenboushi is the process of preventing quality problems before their outbreak (during the design/development stage). Although Mizenboushi has been around for a long period, I credit Tatsuhiko Yoshimura for being the most persistent in its advancement and application. Tatsuhiko wrote about Mizenboushi being made up of several parts (see Figure 10.11). GD^3 is one of the key parts.

Good design corresponds to "use robust" and "make robust" (steps 2 and 3) from the previously described four-step creation process shown in Figure 10.6. Good design is the selection of a design with the fewest number of known issues. Reusing current robust designs is the easiest and cheapest method to achieve good designs. If robust designs are not available, or if the robustness of the designs is unknown, then the use of DFSS and DOE is required to create robust designs.

As illustrated in Figure 10.12, even the most robust design has hidden issues that could generate customer concerns. These buds of problems are the result of the hundreds or even

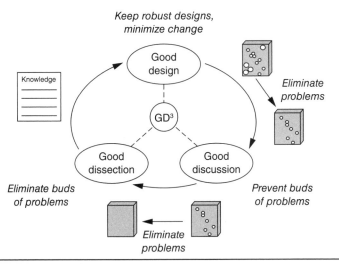

Figure 10.11   GD³.

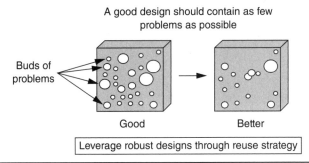

Figure 10.12   Good design.

thousands of individual engineering steps required to make a design, as well as the thousands of noise and control factors that contribute to the production stability of the design.

Hidden issues in the robust design can be significantly reduced with good discussion, followed by good dissection. *Good discussion* is the process of finding and eliminating the buds of problems that remain in robust designs through review and discussion of changes that occur during the design and development process. Special consideration is given to those

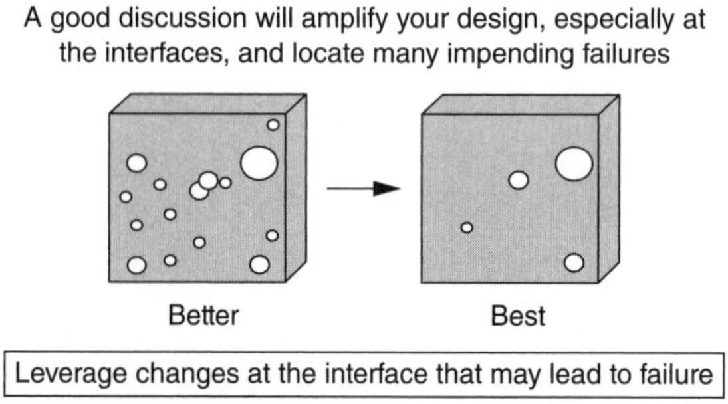

A good discussion will amplify your design, especially at
the interfaces, and locate many impending failures

Better   Best

Leverage changes at the interface that may lead to failure

Figure 10.13 Good discussion.

changes at the interfaces between parts/systems, as well as the
interfaces between organizations (such as engineers, suppliers,
and manufacturing). This is accomplished by creating "good
discussion" with all appropriate engineers, designers, suppliers, and manufacturers (see Figure 10.13).

The discussion of the buds is facilitated in a DRBFM
(design review based on failure modes). The DRBFM builds
on the original DFMEA. The DRBFM concentrates the critical
discussion at the interface between components and systems,
with emphasis on design changes.

These changes may be the result of changes in application,
manufacturing processes, suppliers, and so forth. Changes to
the levels or types of noise and control factors should also be
reviewed during the DRBFM. The objective is to find the buds
of problems that remain in the design. Countermeasures are
planned for all buds found. The results of the discussion are
recorded in a tabulated matrix, as shown in Figure 10.14. A tabulated matrix creates specific action plans that, when followed,
create a design with a minimum number of buds of problems.

Going back to the illustration of GD^3, following the good
discussion, there are still some remaining buds of problems.
These must be reduced through the use of good dissection (see
Figure 10.15). *Good dissection* is the complete review and discussion of the testing and validation to glean as much information as possible.

Part name/ part change or effect of changed environment	Function of the part	Points of concern related to the change		Cause of failure mode/concern		Effect on customer	
			Any other concern (review)	Cause of failure mode/ concern	Any other cause (review)	On customer or system	Severity
D	D	D		D		D	
			R	R	R	R	R

Design actions to eliminate concerns (provide details and best practices used)	Recommended actions (results of review)					
	Design to include	Response/ target	Evaluation to include	Response/ completion date	Production to include	Response/ target
D						
	R	R	R	R	R	R

D = input from the design engineer
R = response from the review team

Figure 10.14   DRBFM.

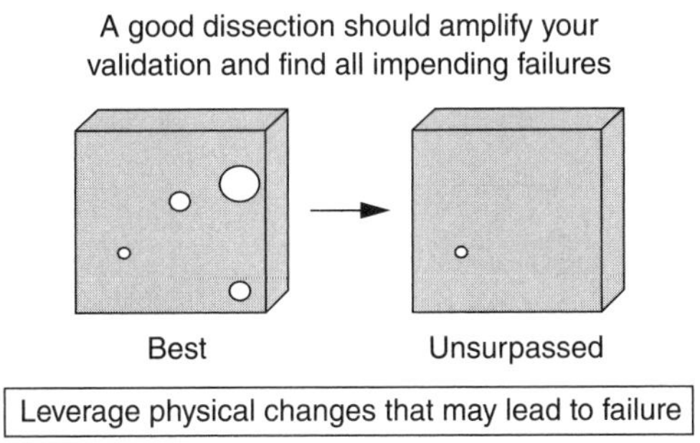

A good dissection should amplify your
validation and find all impending failures

Best   Unsurpassed

Leverage physical changes that may lead to failure

Figure 10.15   Good dissection.

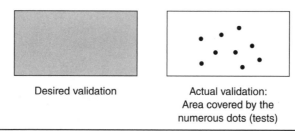

Desired validation   Actual validation:
                                      Area covered by the
                                      numerous dots (tests)

Figure 10.16   Classical validation effectiveness.

As illustrated in Figure 10.16, the purpose of validation is to completely color-in the box (confirm with complete confidence that the design is robust). In actuality, validation colors-in very little of the box.

The reasons for not completely coloring-in the box are mostly due to the statistical limitations of validation testing: Sample sizes are small due to the cost of prototype parts and testing, tests are often not run to failure, and discussions and corrections occur only for observed failures.

Just as the design is reviewed immediately after it is completed, the validation results should be reviewed immediately after the validation test. The purpose of the DRBTR is to review not just the actual failures but also the potential or impending failures. Step one is to review all test failures. Step two is to discuss and review all pending failures, which are identified by reviewing all changes to the physical properties of each system. For each change, the question must be asked, if the test were run longer or harder, would a failure occur? If it could, then this potential failure must also be eliminated.

Looking at Figure 10.17, although we still have not completely colored-in the box, significantly more buds of problems have been discovered and eliminated.

Again, the results of the discussion are recorded in a tabulated matrix (see Figure 10.18). The tabulated matrix creates specific action plans that, when followed, create a design with a minimum number of buds of problems.

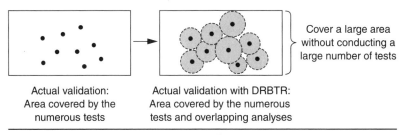

Actual validation: Area covered by the numerous tests

Actual validation with DRBTR: Area covered by the numerous tests and overlapping analyses

Cover a large area without conducting a large number of tests

Figure 10.17 Improved validation effectiveness.

Analysis of test results/observations

Specific area of part	Test results/ observations	Compare with past results from similar tests	Probable cause of results/observations
T	T/R	T/R	T/R

Possible progression of events leading to potential customer complaint	Severity (1, 2, 3, 4)	Problem #	Suggestion by test/validation for review
T/R	T/R	T/R	T/R

Recommended actions per review based on test results

Design/Evaluation/Manufacturing Each observation/suggestion must be addressed and closed	Owner and target date	Closure
R	R	R

T = input from the test engineer
R = response from the review team

Figure 10.18 DRBTR.

Correcting the impending problems or buds of problems associated with the DRBTR completes the "keep robust" portion of the four steps to robustness. The one remaining event that must take place is the documentation of lessons learned and identification of best practices for future designs (see Figure 10.19).

Most knowledge comes from the actual experiences we gain in our journey. The learning generated through the GD[3]

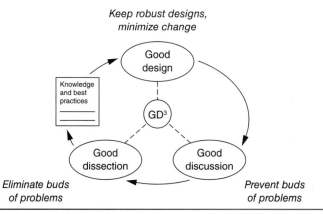

Figure 10.19 GD³—lessons learned.

process must be documented and communicated to ensure the next round of robustness begins where the last concluded.

Creation is the final category of quality initiatives and is the most significant. Creation is about robustness. It is about the process of making new designs that are insensitive to customer variation. Robustness is also about making designs that are insensitive to build and manufacturing variation. Obtaining truly robust designs requires selecting designs that are currently robust, making them even more robust, and then keeping them robust.

ADDITIONAL READING

Chowdhury, S. 2001. *Power of Six Sigma*. Chicago: Dearborn Trade.

———. 2005. *Design for Six Sigma: The Revolutionary Process for Achieving Extraordinary Profits*. Chicago: Kaplan Business.

Yoshimura, T. 2002. *Toyota Style Mizenboushi (Preventative Measures) Method—GD³: How to Prevent a Problem Before It Occurs.* [In Japanese.] Tokyo: JUSE Press.

PART IV
Application

11

Leadership

A pioneering architect in the science of managing for quality, Joseph M. Juran passed away February 28, 2008, at the age of 103. Known as the father of quality, he stated, "It is most important that top management be quality-minded. In the absence of sincere manifestation of interest at the top, little will happen below."

In June 1980, NBC broadcast the program *If Japan Can . . . Why Can't We?*, in which the United States was introduced to W. Edwards Deming and his no-nonsense drive for quality. It is amazing that people today still ask the question "Why can't we?" but fail to seek the wisdom to answer it. Your quality plan can begin and grow only through strong leadership that is unwavering in its goal of winning the race in quality and always asking, "Why can't we?"

I define success as growing a profitable business. To grow a profitable business, you must do a better job than your competitors of satisfying your customers. Satisfying customers requires you to be successful in your quality journey. This journey will not be measured by the knowledge and expertise of your quality experts but by the ability of your leadership to institutionalize knowledge into daily actions by the entire organization. Success is not about great "quality" people; success is about ordinary people executing great quality every day.

The book *The Class of 1846* provides insight into what separates great leaders from mediocre leaders. Over the years, West Point (as well as the other service academies) has produced many great leaders. In *The Class of 1846*, John C. Waugh looks at this class and its later contributions to the most critical time in American history, the Civil War. It is interesting to note that all the leaders had the same training and experiences during their West Point stay. Most had their first experiences in the art of war during the Mexican–American War and in the American Indian Wars, but not all were equal in their leadership success.

In the 1800s, West Point ranked its cadets by achievement and assigned the most prestigious jobs and honors to the highest-ranked cadets (highest to engineering, next to ordnance, followed by artillery and infantry, and the lowest to the mounted rifles or dragoons). Interestingly, the crucible of the Civil War produced a significantly different ranking. Although most 1846 cadets made the rank of general during the war, the number one cadet in the class, Charles Stewart, only made the rank of colonel (and that was after the war). The second-ranked cadet, George McClellan, made the rank of major general and for a time commanded the entire Union army. Although he was an effective organizer and produced great battle plans, he was not an effective leader in battle. Some of the generals who were lower in West Point rank became excellent battlefield commanders. Thomas "Stonewall" Jackson, arguably one of the best generals of the Civil War, initially was not even nominated for West Point and started near the bottom of the class. Jackson graduated 17th out of a class of 59. Ulysses S. Grant (class of 1843) graduated 21st in a class of 39.

John Waugh identifies several key leadership characteristics that I believe are also relevant to companies striving toward quality leadership. The first characteristic that makes great generals and also great leaders is the will to win, whatever the mission. A great leader must have an absolute, unbreakable, unbending passion to succeed no matter what obstacles or roadblocks are found in the journey. A great leader must have cool judgment and be immune to panic. He or she must have the ability to anticipate events and have a plan, but be willing to abandon that plan instantly if it isn't working or if the circumstances require it. The great leader must know the enemy (or competition) and what the enemy is likely to do. The leader must have magnetism or charisma and must stir the enthusiasm and devotion in the troops by setting an example. He or she must move fast and use common sense. And finally, a great leader must win. George McClellan had most of the qualities of a great general, but he failed to win.

Great tools and initiatives are useless unless driven by senior leadership and engaged by the entire organization. Senior leadership must train, coach, and mentor the quality initiatives. Our lives are crammed full of everyday needs and concerns. We are constantly at the mercy of the urgent and have a hard time finding time for the important. It is leadership's responsibility to help us sort out the difference. Leadership must provide the knowledge of and support for the quality journey. No business is ever successful without great leadership. Likewise, no business will be successful in quality without great leadership trained and educated in quality strategy and tools.

Whereas the first characteristic is the will to win, the second characteristic is the knowledge and understanding of the science of war (in our case, the science and understanding of quality). No nation would send its troops to war without leaders trained and experienced in the science of war. There are plenty of great leaders in business and sports, but few with the experience and knowledge required to lead a successful military campaign. Likewise, not just any great leader can be successful in driving quality within a business. And unfortunately, even among quality experts, few have the leadership qualifications to drive a quality transformation in a business.

I once worked for a man named Don Mitchell. Don had spent his career in manufacturing, leading men and machines in a plant environment. He was pulled out of that job and made the head of quality. Although he dealt with quality on a daily basis at the plant, he was mature enough to know that a transformation of an entire company would take more knowledge than what his experiences had given him. With this reflection on his ability to be successful, Don embarked on a mission to learn about quality. He enrolled in Certified Quality Engineer training from ASQ, and to his credit spent the four hours in examinations to verify he understood quality. Don went on to learn about Red X from Shainin LLC and studied the CDC for hints on improving the performance of the quality plan. Don's leadership and quality knowledge allowed him to drive his company to a new level of quality and customer enthusiasm.

During my career I have had numerous opportunities to present detailed quality plans to senior leaders of various companies. Many of these plans had superb quality insight but often did not produce the desired results. Unfortunately it took many years for me to learn that it is not the high-level, sophisticated plans that produce the best results, but rather the simple, executable plans for the common worker. The best plans are just pieces of paper unless the entire organization (especially the leadership) understands the plan and is committed to its implementation.

As stated earlier in the book, one of the best executions of APAT strategies I have seen was the improvement in employee safety at a particular Fortune 500 company. This company determined that its employee safety was not at the level its employees expected and deserved. This company went about outlining that safety would be an overriding expectation of the entire organization. Goals were established and communicated to the entire organization. Regular tracking against those goals was started, and people were appraised on achievement of those goals. The top injury-causing activities were identified and eliminated (focus strategy). Next, every operation that could generate an injury was identified and modified (APAT strategy). Financial needs were drawn up for all safety changes and corrections. The finances were not used to defeat the initiatives but to ensure that the money was being spent wisely. Safety behaviors changed: People now looked at safety as something they needed to be aware of continuously instead of just during the final days before the monthly safety meeting. No meeting or activity was held without first reviewing the actions to be taken in case of an emergency, such as a fire or a tornado. Emergency numbers were posted and response teams created. Within a couple of years, this company moved from average employee safety to one of the best. Although some support was initially obtained from outside, the majority of the improvement was derived from the actions of senior leadership setting the example, creating a strategy, supporting the employees, and expecting a change in behavior and improved results.

This same model can be applied to your quality journey. You typically don't need more strategies; you need more understanding and commitment of how to implement the currently existing strategies. But first you must have the leadership commitment to understanding and driving quality.

As a leader in your company, you are responsible for establishing where your company will end its journey. Will it be mediocre or will it be great? Will you follow the easy path that most businesses are taking, or will your company aim for the pinnacle and set the standard for the industry? Will you provide the leadership to drive the effort required to achieve success?

Your quality journey starts with the desire to be the best. Without the knowledge of your destination and the passion to achieve it, your company will probably travel in an ever-diverging circle without a clear goal or purpose. You must establish quality initiatives and strategies to meet the challenge. But remember that quality will never be achieved by total reliance on a multitude of quality experts. At the same time, you will never have quality greatness with strong leaders who have no quality expertise or experience. You and your leaders must take the time and effort to become knowledgeable in application and execution. I was told that one very successful Korean automotive manufacturer required every executive, including the president of the company, to go through two weeks of DFSS quality training. I am sure that upon completion of the training the president was not able to directly apply the knowledge he had gained, but I am sure he was able to better support the engineers and technicians who were applying it.

Set your goal to be the best in a reasonably short time period. Make sure you are committed to the challenge and prepared for the hardship associated with the journey. Communicate the goal often and convincingly. Reward your employees based on driving and following the plan. Do not let temporary setbacks stand in the way of your goal. Regroup, refocus, and learn from the experience. Don't waste the failures; they provide valuable learning. Remember, you have already paid for this learning, so take full advantage of it. Surround yourself with a few quality experts. Make sure they are not just book smart but experience wise. Make sure they know how to improvise. Send them into the field to get their hands dirty. As Tatsuhiko Yoshimura is always telling me, go for Genchi, Genbutsu ("Go to the place and see the thing").

Leadership must drive the message of fast and significant results. The most significant and rapid improvement makes the most significant headlines. Slow or insignificant improvement only provides the vision of a company that does not care about quality. All quality programs and plans will stagnate over time. Anticipate the stagnation and prepare to break through to the next level of quality. Dr. Yoshimura teaches that when things are starting to look bleak in your quality plan, then "break through." A *breakthrough* is moving from your current position to a more desirable position (see Figure 11.1). Don't hesitate to drive a breakthrough if your results become bogged down. Plan for it. Do not let a stationary quality plan stand in the way of the level of achievement you desire.

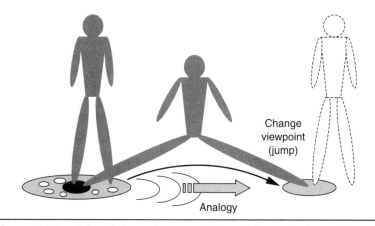

Figure 11.1 A breakthrough connects two things at a long distance.

Drive breakthroughs by setting higher and ever-increasing goals; drive to reduce failures by 50%, and when that is achieved, reduce them again by 50% (or double a metric and double the metric again). To accomplish this you must have a good understanding of your current situation and have the passion to improve. As I discussed earlier with the logistic curve, most companies have run through periods of rapid improvement and are now in a period of stagnation, possibly below their competitor's level (see Figure 11.2).

This situation is normal and unfortunately often accepted. When in this stagnation period, you have three choices: (1) accept the stagnation, (2) improve, or (3) reinvent (see Figure 11.3).

Accepting the stagnation implies acceptance of second- or third-place standing in your business and with your customer. This position will probably result in the slow loss of customers and business, with the possible exception of a monopoly, where you are guaranteed customers.

In most businesses, accepting mediocrity means that over time you will be out of business. Reinvention sounds glamorous and has been successful in some cases, but it requires time and periods of regrowth. Your customers may not wait. For most

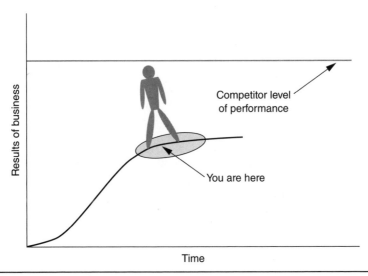

Figure 11.2 Current situation.

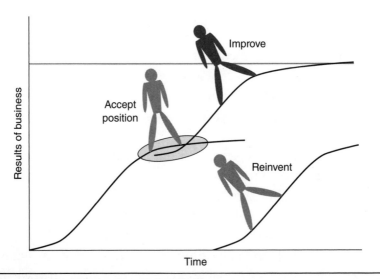

Figure 11.3 Where are you headed?

businesses, success comes from improving the business, not reinventing it.

Now that you want to break through to a new level of quality, how do you go about it? Start by understanding where you are and look for ideas on how to improve (see Figure 11.4).

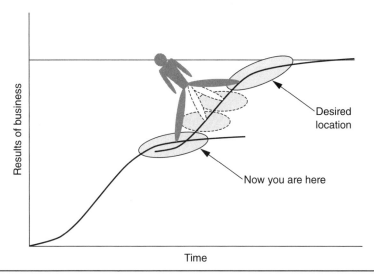

Figure 11.4   Right foot on the current situation, left foot looks for a new area.

Movement to this new and higher level of performance requires a breakthrough, and a breakthrough requires strong leadership. To break through, you will need to give your organization conflicting and high targets (such as higher quality at a lower cost).

Innovation is the result of achieving two or more conflicting targets. Thomas Edison was interested in inventing a filament that not only shown brightly but also lasted for a long duration. This is innovation, or a breakthrough. Do not make trade-offs too easily. If you do, your people may lose the opportunity to make a breakthrough.

If your targets are too low, your people will not drive hard enough for the breakthrough. At the same time, if they are too high, defeatism may set in. It is important to challenge your people with conflicting targets. A recent example of breakthrough is in hybrid vehicles. Two manufacturers came out with hybrids at about the same time, one for buses and one for cars. In both cases the teams had been challenged to double the fuel economy. That target was felt to be impossible, but management was unwavering and the goal was achieved.

The next step is to look for ideas for breakthroughs. For this you will have to call your people together and lead them in a breakthrough workshop. The objective of the workshop is to produce 200 ideas that have the potential of achieving your improvement. You can easily come up with several ideas, but remember that your competitors may have also found these same ideas. Think as though you have 100 competitors in the world. Two hundred ideas probably will mean driving your usual thinking by a factor of 10. If you can produce 20 ideas, you must produce 200 ideas. You must force your people to think deeply to produce these 200 ideas.

I had my own experience with breakthrough. The first time I was involved in a breakthrough workshop I came up with what I thought was a profound idea and reviewed it with Tatsuhiko Yoshimura. He agreed that the idea was profound and then said nothing more. The silence was broken when he asked for the other 199 ideas. Tatsuhiko was right: Anyone could have come up with that great idea, but it would take significant effort to come up with 200 profound ideas. That significance is what often separates companies.

Generating 200 ideas will require your leadership. You will have to help your people think differently. If they think too narrowly, you will have to assist them in thinking more objectively. If they think too widely, you will have to assist them in thinking in a more focused or concentrated way. Combining concentration with objectivity is the basis for innovation.

Breakthrough is not easy, but it is worth the effort. As Thomas Edison is credited with saying, "Innovation is 1% inspiration and 99% perspiration." The "99% perspiration" means you must challenge your mind and never give up. Your people must nurture a challenging mind-set to achieve the high target you have set. To confront the brutal facts and never give up is to produce a proactive improvement mind-set.

To aid in breakthrough, I use the support tool called COACH, which is great for driving quality leadership. COACH stands for <u>c</u>oncentrate, <u>o</u>bjective, <u>a</u>nd <u>ch</u>allenge. I have found that application of COACH works best in a slightly different order of objective, challenge, and concentration.

Let's start with the objective. The objective is the characteristic that senior management is attempting to drive the organization to. This may be a performance or customer metric that is established to meet the business model. It could be market share, quality target, or performance level. Achieving the objective is what senior leadership celebrates. When determining your objective, ask yourself whether management will rejoice (will the customers rejoice?) when you are successful.

The challenge is the value of the metric that is associated with the objective. It could be market share, problems per million products, or some satisfaction metric. The challenge is the level at which customers perceive a significant change. Typically you want to set a goal of twice as good or 50% fewer issues.

The last characteristic is concentration. Concentration is a method for focusing on new opportunities. Concentration provides the ability to recognize patterns and opportunities in data that are often random or dispersed. As stated in Chapter 4, there are two types of concentration: natural and derived. Natural concentrations occur without any outside influence. Derived concentrations occur because of outside influence.

In your leadership breakthrough, look for both natural and derived concentrations to find even larger opportunities. Use concentration to generate ideas in the breakthrough discussion. These concentrations can provide hints on new and creative strategies to significantly improve your quality processes.

Your destination should be to be the best in quality. No other destination is acceptable. Being the best will drive your actions and conversations. Everyone in your organization must recognize the direction in which the company is headed. Broadcast your goals, initiatives, and strategies frequently and enthusiastically.

The quality journey is about execution; it is not about education. The quality journey is about satisfying the customer and growing your business. A great quote comes to mind: "You can't direct the wind, but you can adjust the sails." Government regulations and changing customer preferences may slow your vessel, but don't spend your time battling something that is unmovable; adjust your sails to take advantage of the opportunity.

> *Leadership authors Fred Fiedler and Martin Chemers stated that "the quality of leadership, more than any other single factor, determines the success or failure of an organization." I would add to that quote that leadership in quality is driven more by determined and unwavering leadership than any other factor. Be the leader that the organization needs and your customers demand.*

ADDITIONAL READING

Tichy, N. 2007. *The Leadership Engine: Building Leaders at Every Level.* New York: Pritchett, LP.

Waugh, J. C. 1999. *The Class of 1846: From West Point to Appomattox: Stonewall Jackson, George McClellan, and Their Brothers.* New York: Ballantine.

Appendix

Statistical Engineering Example

To demonstrate the power of the statistical engineering process, I have added this example. Although it is from the auto industry, the methodology is supportive of any industry or service. The methodology for detecting the root cause of the problem is the same as that used by Sherlock Holmes to find the perpetrator of a crime: Eliminate all the people who did not commit the crime, and whoever is left is the culprit.

Prior to starting this problem-solving project, a small team of four people was formed, and they determined that the issue was not caused by lack of control from the facility or from any of the suppliers (the solution to the problem was not in the first three steps of the six-step problem-solving process). The problem had existed for over six months, and normal problem solving had not been able to solve it.

All projects start with direction from leadership. In this example the plant leadership had established a plant goal of improving quality by 15% (in perspective, I would have suggested a more significant goal). The largest issue as reported by the customers was around the door systems. The plant built three different vehicles, and the vehicle identified as B had the most complaints—the biggest being wind noise (see Figure A.1).

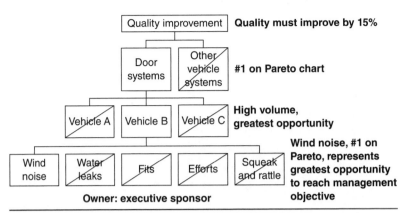

Figure A.1 Preliminary problem definition: the problem as management sees it.

Now that the project had been defined as wind noise in vehicle B, the team needed to determine where in the vehicle the wind noise was most associated. The door with the most wind noise was the right front door. Although the noise was also detected at the left front door, the team solved the problem at the right front door first and then used the solution to fix the left front door. Wind noise at the rear doors was significantly less and was looked at as a separate project later. Looking at the right front door, the team then had to identify where on the door the wind noise was coming from.

Figure A.2 shows the location of point 5. The severity of point 5 could be associated with either wind noise generation or proximity to the passenger's ear—which wasn't important, because either way the customer was not pleased.

Next, determination of the wind noise problem frequencies had to be established. Noise measurements of several BOB and WOW vehicles were taken and the sound spectrum analyzed (see Figure A.3).

The difference in the sound pressure was around 2000 Hz. The difference between the BOBs and the WOWs was about 9 dB of sound pressure. This completes the problem definition: Reduce wind noise for Vehicle B, right front door measured at

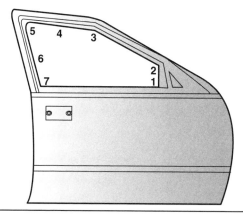

Figure A.2 Microphone locations for checking wind noise at the right front door.

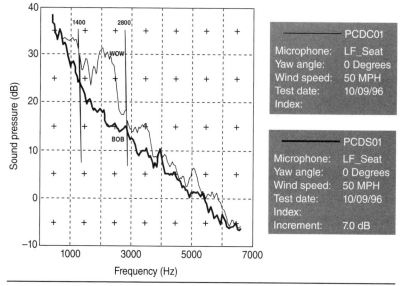

Figure A.3 Sound pressure.

location #5, using B&K 2236, at 2 K filter to below 3 dB, without degrading fits and efforts (see Figure A.4).

The completion of the problem definition step begins the problem solution step. Likewise, the final detail of the problem

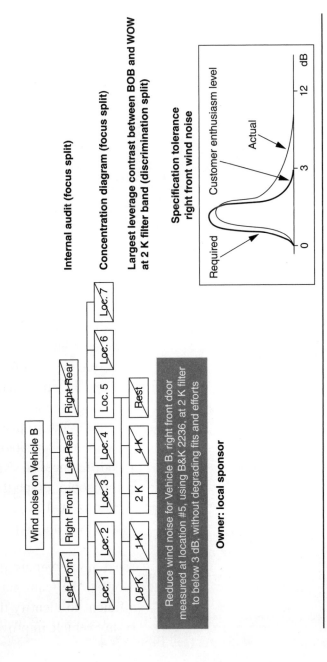

Internal audit (focus split)

Concentration diagram (focus split)

Largest leverage contrast between BOB and WOW at 2 K filter band (discrimination split)

Specification tolerance right front wind noise

Wind noise on Vehicle B

Left Front | Right Front | Left Rear | Right Rear

Loc. 1 | Loc. 2 | Loc. 3 | Loc. 4 | Loc. 5 | Loc. 6 | Loc. 7

0.5 K | 1 K | 2 K | 4 K | Best

Reduce wind noise for Vehicle B, right front door measured at location #5, using B&K 2236, at 2 K filter to below 3 dB, without degrading fits and efforts

Owner: local sponsor

Customer enthusiasm level

Required

Actual

0   3   12   dB

Figure A.4 Problem definition tree.

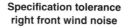

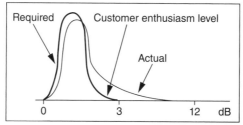

Figure A.5 Right front door wind noise solution tree: objective.

definition is the first detail of the problem solution strategy (see Figure A.5).

The next step was determining a consistent means of measuring the wind noise, vehicle to vehicle. In this case, the plant had a small track next to its assembly operations (see Figure A.6).

Due to the effect of ambient wind speed and direction on the wind, vehicles were recorded around the entire loop and then averaged over time. With this measurement system in place, 30 vehicles were measured twice to determine the repeatability of the measurement system to identify differences in wind noise across vehicles. Figure A.7 shows the isoplot graph that was made. The first run was plotted on the horizontal axis, and the second run was plotted on the vertical axis. This graph is called an isoplot.

By looking at the change in product noise versus the change in measurement noise on the isoplot, the team got a ΔP to ΔM ratio of 8.8. This ratio is sufficient to identify the system as repeatable and able to identify any vehicle improvements made.

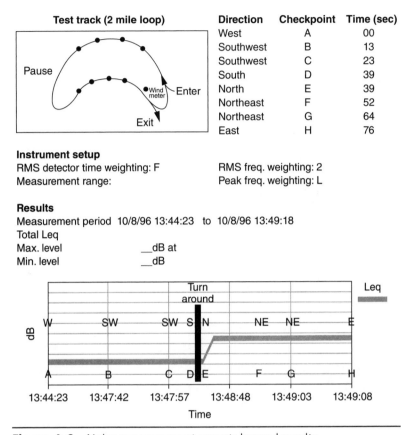

Figure A.6 Noise measurement report: logged results.

It is of interest to point out on the isoplot the large number of good vehicles and the small number of poor vehicles. Often it is at this time that some manager decides to redesign the vehicle or the door system. Before you give in to that temptation, please ask why most vehicles are good and some are bad when they are all produced on the same line, using the same process and the same parts. Do you know enough about the physics of the failure to make a proper change? Here is where statistical engineering can provide not only a solution to the problem but knowledge of the physics of door systems.

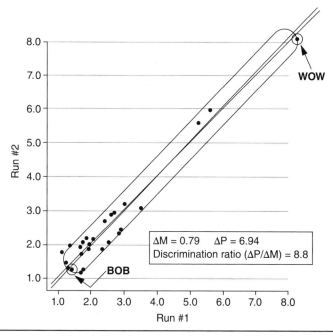

Figure A.7 Isoplot: B&K 2236, 2 K, suction cup fixture.

Since they now had a repeatable measurement system, the team crossed off measurement error as an issue and proceeded with problem solving (see Figure A.8).

The next step is to determine whether the problem was created by the assembly plant in assembling the parts into the vehicle or by the parts that were shipped to the plant.

One way to determine whether the Red X was in the parts or in the assembly is to disassemble and reassemble the door system. Make sure the process for reassembling the door is exactly the same as that done in production. It is best to have the operators who assembled the door do the disassembly and reassembly. This should be done three times, using the door systems from the best vehicle and the worst vehicle (see Figure A.9).

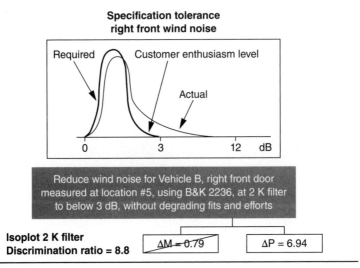

Figure A.8 Right front door wind noise solution tree: measurement sufficient.

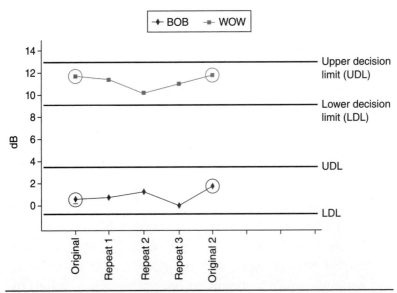

Figure A.9 Location #5: wind noise measured at the 2 K band.

If the best vehicle stays the best and the worst vehicle stays the worst, you have statistical confidence that the problem is within the parts and not in the assembly of the parts. This was extremely important because the plant had started to look at how its processing needed to change to correct the problem. The plant process was fine, so the team needed to investigate which part was responsible for the problem. To signify that the assembly process was not responsible for the problem, the team crossed this area off the chart, do you see the dictionary game, the whole vehicle assembly process has just been eliminated at the cause (see Figure A.10).

Since the door comprises many parts, checking one part at a time could be very time consuming. For this reason statistical engineers should look first at the biggest part, the door module (see Figure A.11). To investigate whether the problem resided in the door module, it was removed, reinstalled three times, and then swapped (good module on the bad door and bad module

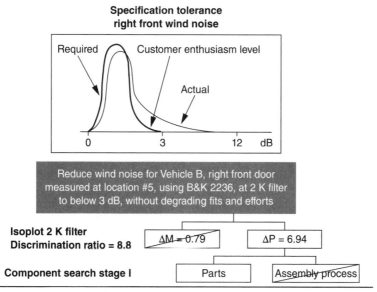

Figure A.10 Right front door wind noise solution tree: solution in the individual parts.

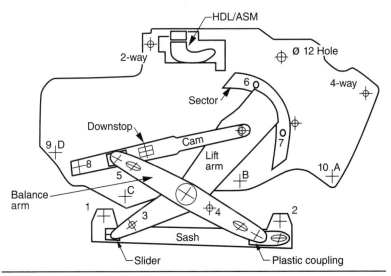

Figure A.11 Right front door window module assembly.

on the good door). Bad module was defined as the door module from the bad door.

When the door module was removed and reinstalled, the BOB vehicles stayed good and the WOW vehicles stayed bad. When the BOB and WOW modules were swapped, the good became bad and the bad became good. Looking at Figure A.12 we can see that wind noise stayed with the door module, not with the rest of the parts in the door system. In this case, the team eliminated every other part in the door as a suspect in the crime of wind noise. (In the dictionary game earlier in the book, a binary search pattern was completed—every question eliminated 50% of the possibilities, and 17 questions were required to identify the word. This example shows that your questioning strategy has the ability to eliminate possible candidates at a faster rate. In the dictionary game, if there were clues that suggested that the word began with "A," then you could have

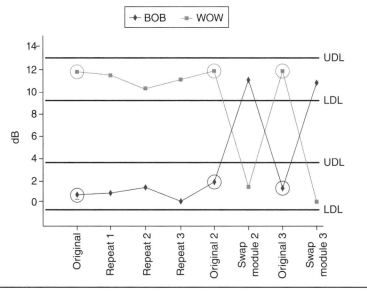

Figure A.12   Location #5: wind noise versus door module.

initially eliminated 115,000 words just by asking whether the word started with an "A.")

The problem lived in the door module (see Figure A.13). Visual inspection revealed no apparent differences between the door modules on the good vehicles and those on the bad vehicles. At this point in the project, the engineer for the door system module identified the points that he thought were critical and that the supplier was measuring and controlling (see Figure A.14).

To do a statistical comparison, five pairs of good door modules and five pairs of bad door modules were measured at the 10 points the engineer had identified (see Table A.1). If any of these points were critical to the problem, there would be a contrast. The points on the good parts would be higher or lower as a group than the points on the bad parts. Looking

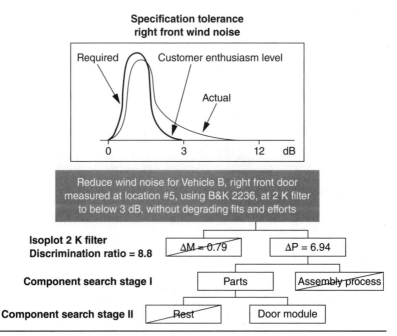

Figure A.13 Right front door wind noise solution tree: solution in the door module.

at all 10 points showed no contrast. Some were higher, some lower. No patterns were detected. It was interesting that the expert thought these 10 points were critical when there was something else that was even more critical that the expert was unaware of.

Not finding any contrasts within the door modules but knowing that the Red X lived in the door module created an interesting problem. It was at this stage that the team needed more clues. To generate these clues, the team returned to the assembly plant floor. The best source for clues was the assemblers. Every day they build hundreds of vehicles, so they can often tell what makes good and bad vehicles. In this case the operator noticed that if he held one end of the door module up higher when he installed it, the vehicle seemed to have less

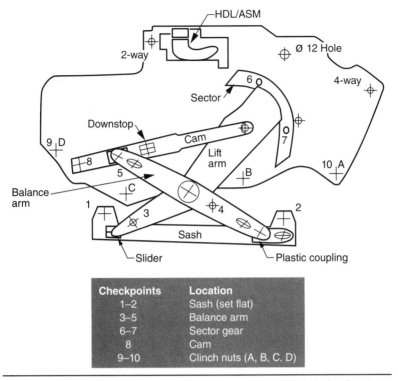

Figure A.14 Coordinate measurement machine (CMM) checkpoints: right front door window module assembly, checkpoints for paired comparison—in "ship" position.

wind noise. To evaluate this on the door modules, the team went back and looked at the relative differences between the vertical height on two distant points (points 1 and 2). When a comparison was made of the sash tilt (difference in height between points 1 and 2), a contrast was observed. All of the good door modules had sash tilts less than 1.9 mm, while all of the bad door modules had sash tilts larger than 2.6 mm. This contrast suggests that the sash tilt of the door module was possibly a major contributor of wind noise associated with the WOW doors. Table A.1 shows the sash tilt as the last line on the table, which is highlighted.

Table A.1 Group comparison of CMM data for right front door module assemblies; checked in three-quarters-up position, using body coordinates.

Module #	#2	#5	#7	#9	#11	#1	#4	#6	#8	#10	Change/Consistent
BOB/WOW	BOB	BOB	BOB	BOB	BOB	WOW	WOW	WOW	WOW	WOW	
Wind noise (dB) **Green Y**	60.1	58.5	58.8	58.5	58.6	66.9	71.5	70.0	67.5	69.1	
Pt 1 Sash left hole											
X axis fore/aft	3087.7	3088.8	3088.9	3087.8	3088.3	3088.2	3087.8	3086.7	3087.8	3088.5	NO
Z axis up/down	959.7	961.7	962.8	961.0	962.0	965.0	962.7	961.5	962.1	965.4	NO
Pt 3 Slot lower bal arm											
X axis fore/aft	2973.2	2972.7	2972.9	2973.6	2972.3	2972.3	2972.4	2972.9	2973.2	2972.1	TIE
Z axis up/down	889.7	891.4	892.2	890.5	891.6	893.8	892.0	891.1	891.2	894.0	NO
Pt 5 Slot upper bal arm											
X axis fore/aft	2996.0	2995.2	2995.2	2996.4	2994.7	2995.5	2995.4	2995.9	2996.6	2995.4	NO
Z axis up/down	735.6	738.1	735.6	738.8	735.4	736.9	736.7	735.9	736.9	737.4	TIE
Pt 11 Center downstop											
X axis fore/aft	2932.0	2930.2	2930.5	2931.3	2929.7	2931.0	2930.3	2931.1	2932.1	2930.4	NO
Z axis up/down	735.0	735.4	735.2	736.3	735.3	735.9	735.9	735.3	735.7	736.2	NO

← Candidate X's →

Candidate X's											
Pt 8 Cam stud											
X axis fore/aft	3080.4	3078.6	3078.9	3079.7	3078.5	3080.2	3078.9	3079.3	3080.7	3079.4	NO
Z axis up/down	701.7	702.8	702.8	703.7	702.0	702.8	703.7	702.8	703.8	703.6	TIE
Pt 2 Sash right hole											
X axis fore/aft	2702.6	2703.5	2704.0	2702.5	2703.3	2703.6	2702.7	2701.6	2702.7	2703.5	NO
Z axis up/down	958.4	960.4	961.4	959.1	961.1	962.4	959.6	958.7	958.9	962.0	NO
Four way locator											
X axis fore/aft	2442.9	2442.5	2443.3	2443.2	2442.8	2443.0	2443.2	2442.6	2443.0	2443.3	NO
Z axis up/down	862.1	862.1	862.4	862.2	862.5	862.1	862.3	862.2	862.3	862.4	NO
Pt 1 Z axis	959.7	961.7	962.8	961.0	962.0	965.0	962.7	961.5	962.1	965.4	
Pt 2 Z axis	958.4	960.4	961.4	959.1	961.1	962.4	959.6	958.7	958.9	962.0	
Sash tilt (Pt1Z–Pt2Z)	1.3	1.3	1.4	1.9	0.9	2.6	3.1	2.8	3.2	3.4	YES

Table A.2 Rank order characteristic: sash tilt (point 1–point 2) in up position.

Value (mm)	Module	Wind noise
0.9	BOB #11	58.6
1.3	BOB #5	58.5
1.3	BOB #7	58.8
1.3	BOB #2	60.1
1.9	BOB #9	58.5
2.6	WOW #1	66.9
2.8	WOW #6	70.0
3.2	WOW #4	71.5
3.2	WOW #8	67.5
3.4	WOW #10	69.1

Table A.2 clearly demonstrates the associations between door module sash tilt and wind noise.

Although the evidence pointed to the door module sash tilt as committing the crime, the team needed more evidence. In the crime analogy, we need to have a lineup. For the lineup here, the team needed six randomly selected vehicles: three new vehicles with low sash tilt and three with high sash tilt. Three had sash tilts less than 2 mm, and three had sash tilts over 2 mm. The team measured the wind noise for all six doors and rank ordered their findings. A clear separation is identified in Table A.3, and the team was confident that the Red X resided in sash tilt of the door module.

In this case the three vehicles with the most wind noise also had the highest module sash tilt. Those with low tilt had low wind noise. From this the team concluded that window module

Table A.3 A vs. B: right front wind noise.

A sash tilt < 2.0		C sash tilt > 2.0
Rank order of experiments		
Sash tilt	**Level**	**Wind noise**
−0.4	A	0.1
0.1	A	0.0
0.3	A	0.4
3.2	B	6.7
4.6	B	7.3
5.2	B	20.1
Sash tilt is the main contributor.		

sash tilt was the principal cause of wind noise on Vehicle B (see Figure A.15).

These findings are great, but what do you do with this information? Going back to our Five Cs, we need to start containment immediately to protect the customer. We now know that if we measure the sash tilt on all modules, we can eliminate wind noise from Vehicle B. Figure A.16 shows how we need to sort and scrap any module that has more than 2.1 mm of tilt.

You are now protecting your customer, but in the process you have increased the cost to your supplier and maybe to yourself. Scrapping parts always costs money, and someone has to make up for the loss.

The next logical step is to start the problem-solving process again—this time not on wind noise but on window module sash tilt.

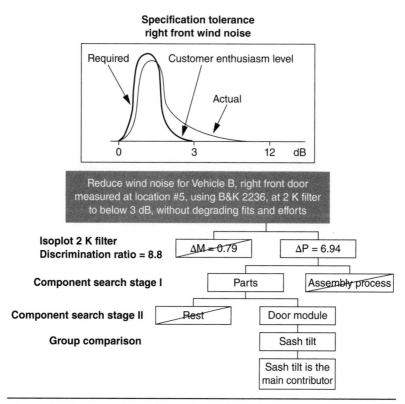

Figure A.15 Right front door wind noise solution tree: sash tilt is the main contributor to wind noise.

This starts phase two of the problem solving: Why do some modules have less than 2.1 mm of tilt while others have significantly more?

Let's first define the problem: reduce sash tilt of the right front door module to less than 2 mm (see Figure A.17).

As before, the first step is to understand the measurement system. Will it be truthful in distinguishing good products from bad products? In the crime analogy, it is very difficult to get great clues from witnesses who are liars. Likewise, if your measurement system is not accurate and repeatable, it is like obtaining clues from a liar. Just like in phase one of

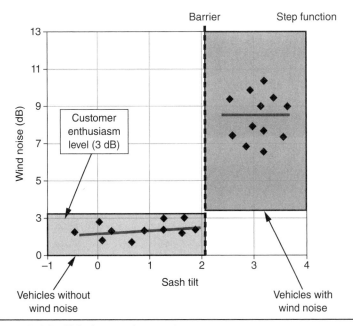

Figure A.16 Window sash containment strategy.

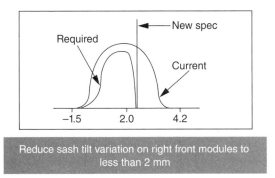

Figure A.17 Solution tree.

our problem solving, we must measure 30 modules twice (see Figure A.18).

These measurements provide a visual display of the repeatability. For this project the discrimination ratio of the product to the measurement system was over 18. This measurement

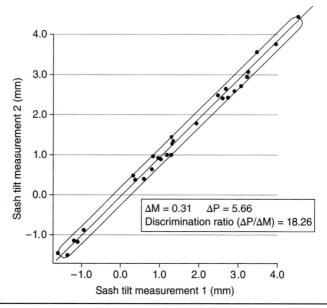

Figure A.18 Sash tilt isoplot.

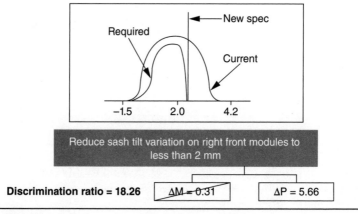

Figure A.19 Solution tree: measurement sufficient.

system is very repeatable and will not lead us astray in our investigation. We can now cross off the measurement system from our problem definition (see Figure A.19).

Just like in the assembly plant, the next step is to determine whether the problem lies in the parts at the module supplier or

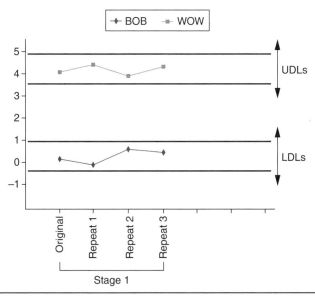

Figure A.20   Component search: right front wind noise, sash tilt in
window module.

in the supplier process for assembling the parts. The module is
disassembled and reassembled three times (see Figure A.20).

In each case the good module (less than 2 mm of tilt) remains
good and the bad module (more than 2 mm of tilt) remains bad.
The problem lies in the parts, not in the assembly of the parts.
In our solution tree we cross off "assembly," indicating that the
problem lies in the components (see Figure A.21).

The next step is to swap the lift arm assembly between the
two modules. In this case, the good module became bad and
the bad module became good (see Figure A.22). This complete
reversal strongly indicates that the problem lies with the lift
arm assembly. If you did not get complete reversal, then the
lift arm assembly could be a problem, but something else is
likely wrong.

Since we do have complete reversal, we have just eliminated every other part within the module. The problem lies with
the lift arm assembly (see Figure A.23).

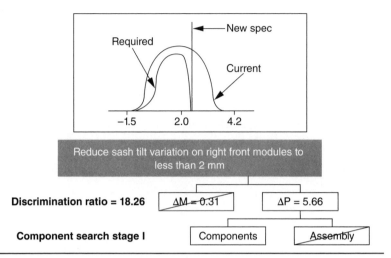

Figure A.21 Solution tree: solution in the parts.

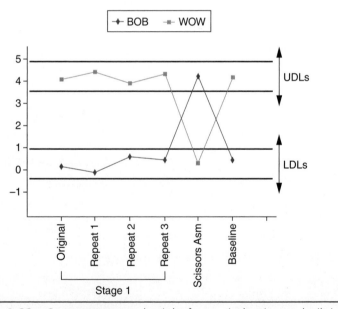

Figure A.22 Component search: right front wind noise, sash tilt in window module.

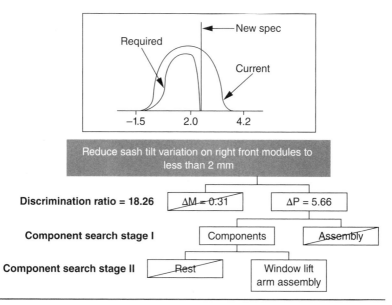

Figure A.23 Solution tree: solution in the lift arm assembly.

The next step is to use a paired comparison to look at the key features of the lift arm assembly. From that analysis (not shown) it was determined that the problem lived within the balance arm. We next did an active multivari analysis and found the problem lived within the welding process of the balance arm. Finally it was confirmed by A vs. B that the problem lived in the clamping of the weld station for the balance arm (see Figure A.24).

Going back to the original problem of wind noise, we can see the tortuous path that was followed to get to the true root cause. Although all problems are not this complex and do not require this magnitude of problem solving, you must ask yourself whether you would have been able to solve this problem if you did not have the tool of statistical engineering. It is unlikely that any brainstorming session or fishbone analysis would have ever identified a weld clamp at a tier 3 supplier as the cause of

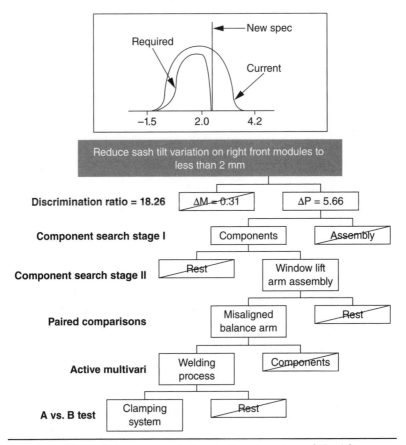

Figure A.24 Solution tree: solution in the clamping of the lift arm assembly.

the wind noise on a completed vehicle. Most work would have been put into inspection and repair, sorting of parts, and lengthy discussions with suppliers without the hope of ever eliminating the problem.

Remember the quote from Dorian Shainin: "Talk to the parts." If you are willing to listen to the parts (and the operators), you will be able to solve even your most difficult problems.

Index

Note: Page numbers followed by f *or* t *refer to figures or tables, respectively.*